A *California Explorer*
Meade Fischer

Five years of articles in *California Explorer* Magazine

July/Aug 2009- July/Aug 2014

First pirnting: July 2014

ISBN: 0-9672523-9-3

Contact: California Explorer Magazine

P.O. Box 1494

Martinez, CA 994553

for subscriptions: 800-833-0159

For Marie Reed, a wonderful editor!

Contents (in chronological order)

Pg

Introduction

It seem no more than a few weeks ago, but looking back on my copies of California Explorer, I realize that I've been writing for them for over five years, and it's definately been a labor of love. After all, what's not to love about going for a hike-- one of my favorite activities-- taking some photos,--another favorite-- and then sitting down at my computer and reminising about the experience.

About the time I read about the Sonoma Mountain addition to Jack London Park, a friend, Warren Rider, who aslo writes occasionally for California Explorer, told me about the magazine and suggested I send my story to them. I dashed off, took a wonderful hike in an unseasonable rain, wrote about it and had it accepted. I've been fortunate to be in all but two or three issues since, something I'd like to contribute to my outstanding prose style, but more likely to an editor who just happens to like what I send.

While the majority of these pieces are about hikes near the Bay Area and the Central Coast, some range from Big Bear to almost the Oregon border and to the Sierra. Most of these aren't difficult, generally half day hikes, but they are all very much worth the effort. They are all scenic and worth bringing a camera along.

As an extra, I've included a few pieces I wrote for my "Out and About" column for the now-defunct Monterey Bay News and Views, another publication that actually paid me to go out and have fun.

I've tried to describe the hikes in enough detail to let the reader know if it's something he or she would enjoy. For each of these hikes, there are at least a hundred others I could have taken, so these were, to me, worth the time spent getting there and hiking. I hope you find these worth your time too.

1. In Searc h of Sonoma Mountain (July/August 2009)

When I read that Mickey Cooke and Pat Eliot, two ladies who have crusaded for six decades to acquire the top of Sonoma Mountain for the public, had finally succeeded, and that it afforded panoramic views of the entire North Bay, I knew I had to get up there and take a look around.

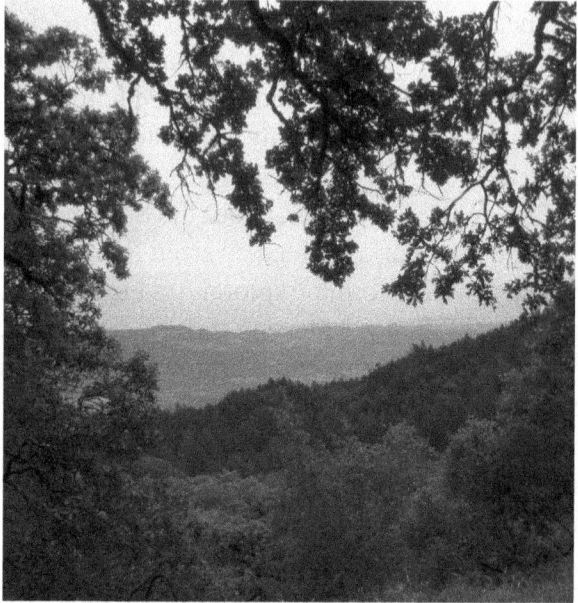

The mountain, saved from development in a $9.95 million deal that closed on Dec. 31, 2008, was purchased when The Sonoma Land Trust, the Sonoma County Agricultural Preservation and Open Space District and the California Coastal Conservancy pooled their resources and bought the 283-acre Sonoma Mountain Ranch.

The mountain, on the spine of the range that separates Petaluma and the 101 corridor from Sonoma and the Valley of the Moon, tops out at around 2,400 feet, no Mt. Whitney, Mt. Denali or even Mt Diablo, it is still one of the highest points in Sonoma County and situated so it offers views of Mt. Tam, Mt. Diablo, plus Mt. Hood and Red Mt. to the north, and even, on a clear day, a touch of the blue Pacific over the hills of Golden Gate National Recreation Area, 360 degrees of some of the Bay Area's finest scenery.

My first instinct was to take the easy way up, so I drove up Sonoma Mountain Road, off Adobe Road, east of Petaluma. After over five miles of twisting road and delightfully bucolic mountain pastures, I came to the end of the road. Unfortunately, there were "no parking" signs, and the road ended at a locked gate topped with rows of barbed wire, along with "no trespassing" signs. After sitting in the car for a few minutes, considering my next move, I started getting the feeling that someone didn't want people accessing the top of the mountain through their land.

Luckily, it was a clear day, so even from below the summit, I could see most of west Sonoma and Marin counties.

After a bit of research I realized that the only way up would be through Jack London State Historical Park near Glen Ellen. Naturally, this couldn't be driven and would involve an eight and a half mile round trip and a 1,800 foot climb. I discovered that, while this top parcel would eventually be part of the park, with official trails and all, the process had not been completed yet. Still, the park boundary was only about a quarter mile from the summit.

I set aside May first to make the trip, camera in hand to catch those spectacular vistas. However, and unusual for May, rain was expected. Thinking a light spring shower wouldn't be a problem, I drove into the park as soon as it opened.

It is quite a straight forward trip up the mountain. Upon paying at the entrance, I turned right to the parking lot for the lake and the London historic farm. In a few dozen yards I passed the old farm buildings and the London Cottage. Then the dirt road split at a vineyard, the main trail to the lake on the right, passing the two silos and rounding the upper end of the vineyard. Then there is a locked gate to stop vehicles and two lake trail options, both the same distance.

The lake is a mile from the parking lot, and it is mostly choked with plants, filled in and much smaller than during London's time. At the lake the Mountain Trail begins, a well maintained dirt road that extends almost to the top of the park. From this point on, it is easy to follow, if not always easy to climb, just stay on the road and follow the Mountain Trail signs for another three miles.

The trail winds up through redwood groves and mixed forests, over several tiny creeks and through some meadows, rich with flowers in the spring. About a half mile above the lake, the trail leaves the woods and enters a small clearing, with huge patches of purple vetch on one side and a mass of yellow lupine on the other. There is a bench facing the Sonoma Valley, and I quickly realized that the park service only puts benches where the views are exceptional, so it is wise to stop, rest and look around.

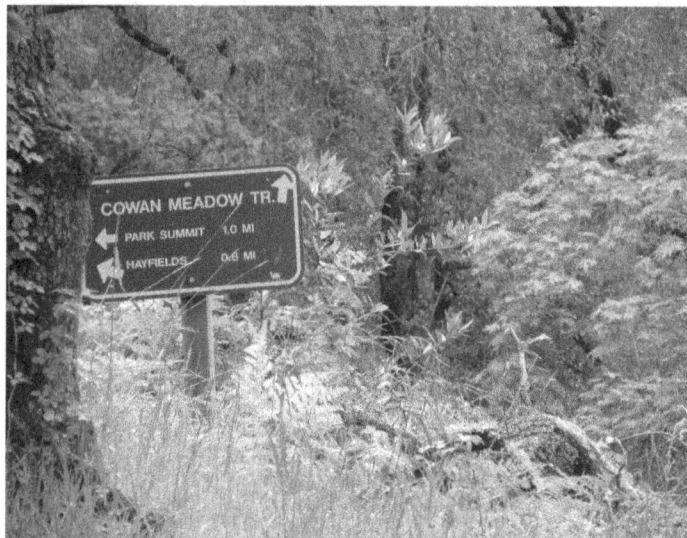

As I continued past the bench, a wild turkey was walking on the path. It kept running ahead of me as I ascended, never re-alizing that stepping off the trail would get it out of my way.

About a half mile further, a trail leads off to the left, through another meadow to Asbury creek, a lovely waterway to follow down, but on another day or possibly on the way back. There are three or four other trail junctions further up, but the Mountain Trail is clearly marked and always on the dirt road.

There's another clearing with another bench, which on a clear day affords a great view of Mt. Diablo. Then the mixed for-est again. Soon the canopy opens up, and scattered oaks are strewn in a thick, verdant, knee deep meadow.

Entering the meadow, I startled a deer, who dashed into the woods and a hawk that was on a limb just above my head.

Since I was the only person on the trail that day, no one had scared the wildlife.

High on the mountain side, it is mostly open meadow with a sprinkling of oaks, and then the trail forks. The right leads to the far end of the park and the hayfields, The left reads "Park Summit .4 mile," almost there. It becomes a single track to the top, running along the park boundry fence for the last couple hundred yards.

On the other side of the fence is the newly acquired property and the summit, an open meadow with no trails. While there are no signs against trespassing, the fence seems to discourage further travel, but since it has been bent and stepped on, it's obvious that people keep hiking.

It's about another quarter mile to the summit, marked with a small pyramid of rocks. Getting there necessitates cutting through thick fields of thistle, grasses and flowers, passing to the left of a fenced microwave relay tower and over the paved access road.

Once on top, the western side of the mountain comes into view, along with west Marin, Mt. Tam. and possibly even the distant ocean. Not on this day. At the top the light sprinkles I'd experienced on the trail up turned into serious rain, and the visibility was reduced to just a few indistinct miles. Due to the weather, the reader can't enjoy the vistas vicariously via my photos.

The curious will just have to spend a day hiking up, preferably on a very clear day.

The weather was a bit kinder on the way down, allowing photos between showers. Fortunately, the downpour that lasted the rest of the day started just as I got back in the car.

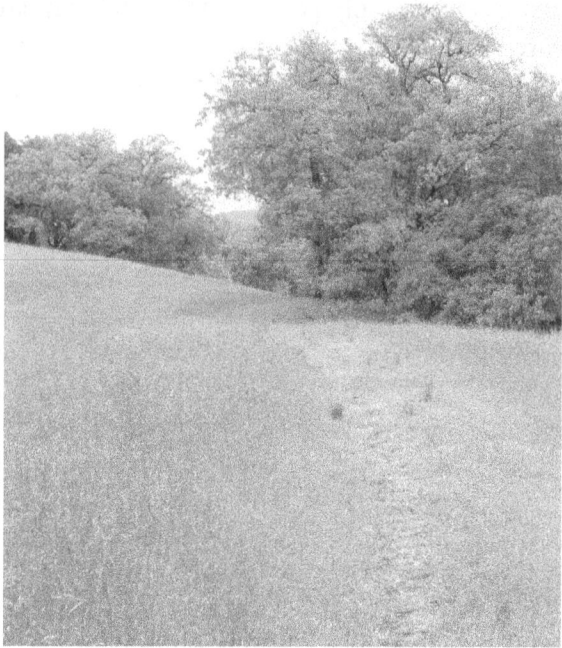

An eight and a half mile hike requires a post hike treat, and while Sonoma is noted for wine, only a good beer satisfies sweaty, tired hikers. Fortunately, Sonoma County's newest microbrewery opened near the end of April. Tim Goeppinger's Sonoma Springs Brewing Co. at 750 W. Napa St. in Sonoma is the perfect place to shake off the dust or mud of the trail.

Getting there: From San Francisco and the south, take 101 to the 37 in Novato, and go east to the 121 (Sonoma exit). When the 121 turns east, continue north on Arnold Drive for 11 miles to Glen Ellen. Arnold Dr. makes a hard right in Glen Ellen, so go to the left, which is London Ranch Road, and the park is at the end of the road.

From the north and Santa Rosa, take hwy. 12 south to Arnold Dr. and in to Glen Ellen.

2 Upward through the Wildflowers (Garland Ranch, Sept/Oct 2009)

There are hiking destinations along California's central coast that attract a dedicated band of regulars. One of these is Garland Ranch Regional Park in Carmel Valley. While there is a hard core of folks who hike and run there weekly, Garland is never more popular than in the spring, when a stunning mix of wildflowers blanket both valley floor and hill sides.

A good way to get a cross section of this 4500 acre park, (with a good selection of the many flowers the park has to offer) is to hike from the river to the top, a half day hike that gives a good aerobic workout and a visual feast.

The park, 8.6 miles on Carmel Valley Road from Highway One in Carmel, starts at the Carmel River. There is parking off the side of the road, and near the parking area is a bridge over the river. Once on the park side of the river, follow the sign to the left for 200 yards to the visitor's center, the best jumping off place for exploring the western end of the park. While there, you can pick up a trail map, fill your water bottle, and take a look at books and charts that list the local flowers and birds.

From the visitor's center, take the trail that leads across the meadow directly toward the thickly wooded hills. In the spring, this meadow is a blinding mix of yellow poppies and blue lupine. As the trail rises, turn left on the Lupine Loop, where you'll see owls clover, blue dicks, vetch, miners lettuce, red clintonia and western blue-eyed grass. Bay and buckeye trees tower over head.

After about a half mile the Lupine Loop trail intersects the Mesa Trail.

Now the climbing begins. In addition to the flowers seen below, you'll start to notice Indian paint brush and the occasional wild iris. When you stop to catch your breath, look down at the valley spread out below you.

At the intersection with the Sky Trail, is the Mesa Trail which leads to the mesa itself, with fields of flowers and a small pond. Or save that for the way down and continue up the Sky Trail, where the Indian paint brush grows in big clumps at almost every turn, mixed with red clintonia and vetch.

I know I said this before, but this is really where the climb seriously begins, and on a hot day it can be strenuous. Make sure you have plenty of water. However, the advantage of this steep trail is that you'll want to stop often to admire the vistas, which expand at every stop.

The top of the Sky Trail is over 1,800 feet, directly above the valley floor. From the small bench at the top, you can see miles of the valley, plus parts of the Salinas Valley over the top of the next range of hills. The top is a hillside meadow, complete with dozens of tiny flowers, a good place to simply lie down in the shade of a tree or in the warmth of the sun and hear the buzzing of thousands of busy insects.

From this vantage point, (the top of Snively's Ridge), you can look south over another valley and to the Ventana range in Big Sur.

On the way down, (if you've already taken a side trip to the Mesa), pick up the Fern Trail. It climbs a bit before heading down a shaded canyon to a charming little pond with a bench, a perfect place to cool off and look for frogs, before heading down to rejoin the Mesa Trail.

Getting There: From Northern Calif, take 101 past Gilroy to the 156, five miles to Hwy 1 and continue south past Monterey to Carmel Valley Road in Carmel. Turn left and the park is 8.6 miles on the right. From So. Calif., take 101 to the Hwy 68 exit in Salinas. Take 68 to Hwy 1, and go south to Carmel Valley Road. Also, coming from the south, and for a totally stunning drive along one of the most scenic back roads in Central California, exit the 101 at G 16 at Greenfield, and take it to Arroyo Seco where it becomes Carmel Valley Road.

3. Tomales Point: A fog shrouded mystery (Nov./Dec. 2009)

The five mile hike to the end of Tomales Point at Point Reyes National Seashore is a delight almost any time, but in mid-summer, when the fog blows in from the ocean in roiling billows, it can be almost mystical.

That was how it was my first time.

Once on the Point Reyes peninsula, the road branches, and the majority of people head south toward the lighthouse. I headed north toward McClure's Beach. Just past the beach the road ends at the Historic Pierce Point Ranch, well preserved, and interesting in its own way. However, the magic begins behind the ranch, on the seaward side, where the trail departs.

That day, with hot weather inland, a 20 knot wind was blowing waves of for over the point. I stepped out, and within a few yards, the ranch had disappeared. Visibility was in feet and yards. Every couple of minutes the fog would clear for just a moment, revealing some piece of brilliant scenery. Captured as if by a strobe light, it was printed like a photo on the eyes and the brain. I could see faint traces, like the pencil lines barely visible under a watercolor, and then suddenly the scene emerged in bright sunlight for just a moment before closing off again and opening in some other direction a minute later. Sometimes it would be the ocean side, steep cliffs and a thundering sea, while at other times it would be the gentle hills rolling down to placid Tomales Bay and the village of Marshall across the water.

This constant shifting of views, this juxtaposition of the wild shore and the placid shore, made this more than just a hike. It made it more like an excursion into the nature of the human thinking process. We think in opposites: night and day, right and wrong, poor and rich, civilized and wild. One view was of one of the wildest pieces of coast, the other of rolling hills and boats bobbing on a bay. I was lost in the constant interplay, always trying to guess what scene would appear next.

Once as the fog cleared, I passed a herd of grazing tule elk. This is a reserve for these splendid animals. As I crested a hill, I saw, just off the trail, something waving in the wind. Something that did not look like the low shrubs and grasses that cover most of the point. I stepped off the trail for a closer look, and emerging from the fog was a very large skunk, waving its tail excitedly at me. It was warning me that he was there and prepared to ruin my day. Then I realized that it was downwind on a blustering day, and I would have had to walk around him to get sprayed. I stepped within 10 feet of the nervous animal before I backed off, not from fear, but from respect for a creature whose home I was invading.

There was a deeply eroded canyon just off the trail, a small creek trickling down it, undoubtedly ending at the unseen beach. I stepped off the trail and to the edge, thinking I could go no further. Then, another short stretch of trail appeared, and I went to the next "dead end." It only opened to another piece of trail. Before long, I was almost on the beach, having spiraled down into what seemed like a fractal. The complexity of the scenery was growing as I worked my way down. Finally, the dark indentations I noticed from above were now above me, and they were deep caves, These caves were large enough to be home for the mountain lions and coyotes that live in the area.

The trail runs along the spine of the point and drops into the only grove of trees. This is at a low spot, with standing water about three miles out. Beyond this, the trail rises to Tomales Bluff and turns to sand. The trail actually separates into several trails that meander out toward the end of the bluff.

At one clearing, Bird Rock flashed into view, vivid in the summer sun. The birds were caught in mid flight, the bright greens and oranges of the lichen and ice plant visible along the broken cliff, and brilliant white waves exploded on the rocks. Then it was gone, and the town of Dillon Beach, with the RV campgrounds rose from beyond Tomales Bay and beyond the tan summer grasses that sloped gently down to the bay. By this time, I was fascinated with the constant shifting between opposites, and then I remembered that this was the place where the Pacaific tectonic plate meets the North American. This point was the last finger of land, the leading edge of thousands of miles of plate, including southern California and all of Baja. It resembled the prow of a massive lithic ship, steaming north at two inches per year, bound for a union with Alaska several million years from now.

As my imagination played with this idea, and as the scenes alternated, I started to wonder how this hike would resolve itself. Would I end on some bay side beach or scrambling down a steep cliff to a wave-swept cove? Curiosity made me quicken my step. The vegetation had changed on the final section of the trail. Once in sand, I was walking through dune habitat in soft sand. I was getting so close to the end that when the fog cleared, I could see both sides of the point without turning my head.

Then, suddenly, the trail split, the right fork descended a few yards to the bay side. The left split to a steep drop toward wave-washed rocks. Straight ahead of me Bodega Head drifted faintly in and out of the fog, and just below me the bluff ended at a huge slab of rock. It was just above the water line, rivulets of white water running off it after each wave. This most inhospitable spot was hearth and home to a flock of various seabirds. I sat and watched this scene, this fitting end to a rost magical hike.

On another trip, a friend and I launched our kayaks from the ramp at Marshall, paddled across Tomales Bay past Hog Island and into White Gulch. After pulling the kayaks above the high tide line, we bushwhacked in a zigzag pattern up the steep hill toward the trail. On the way, we almost walked through a large herd of elk. While they normally ignore people, we were not in the usual place. They kept moving off, always looking back to see what mischief we were up to. We finally located the trail almost a mile in from the ranch and continued toward the point. This was in early fall, the point was warm, almost free of wind and completely fog free. The views were stunning, the weather comfortably warm, the hike relaxing, but without the fog some of the magic was missing.

Each time I take this hike, I explore something I had missed the time before. There are coves and pocket beaches, and a rich assortment on animal life, hiking in the fog just yards from the trail.

While there, be sure to wander thought Historic Pierce Point Ranch. Each building has a sign explaining its history and use. Also, just before the ranch, a short trail leads to McClures's beach, a great place to watch the raw forces of nature

Getting there: Take Highway One through Marin, turn west on Sir Francis Drake Blvd, between Olema and Point Reyes Station. Stay on Sir Francis Drake as it curves to the right and continue through the little town of Inverness. Turn right on Pierce Point road, continuing on to the ranch at the end.

4. Coast Ridge Road: It's about the view (March/Apr. 2010)

Trails invite the hiker for several reasons: Exercise, exploration or an exotic destination. Probably one of the biggest draws is scenery. For those who search for inspiring vistas, there is a hike along Big Sur's ridges that will print panoramas on the memory chip of the mind. This is the section of the North Coast Ridge Road from the Ventana Inn to Timber Top and down to Highway One.

Within a fifteen minute walk from the parking lot, the vistas open up, and for the rest of the hike there are 180 to 360 degree views of the Big Sur Coast and the rugged Ventanas.

This hike, somewhere between nine and ten and a half miles, is unpaved and almost totally resident access and fire road, and while there is something charming and other worldly about looking down at a blanket of summer fog that stretches to the horizon, the real panoramas are reserved for the late fall through early spring. Clear windy days and days after a rain offer the best conditions, days when the farthest peaks seem close enough to grab.

While one can walk up the ridge and return the same way, the full hike requires at least two vehicles and a short shuttle. Drive past the Big Sur valley to Coast Gallery and continue about 500 yards. There are some old stock pens on the inland side of the road, along with room to park a few cars. Leave a ve-hicle there and go back north about five miles to the Ventana Inn. Go up the hill, and park in the lower lot, below the inn and restaurant. If you feel like splurging, eat at the inn, and if you feel like seriously splurging, rent a room for the night. The parking lot is just before a gate, where it becomes a dirt road.

Only the few residents on the ridge and the forest service are allowed to drive the road. It's a wide, dirt road with a gentle to moderate grade, a steady uphill for about four miles to the top of the ridge. At 2,600 feet, where the road undulates, it climbs slightly to Timber top at about 3,000 feet.

By mile one the vistas open. The Ventana Inn lies just below, and the Post Ranch is just west of the highway. By mile two, there are views up the coast to Point Sur and the lighthouse, along with Mount Manual, just north of the gorge. The massive 4,000 foot mountain looms over the Pfeiffer Big Sur State Park. Then the road turns south again, and there is the first view of the rugged peaks of the Ventana, and on a clear day they seem only yards away.

The road continues to climb and twist, offering views almost straight down to the ocean, past grass-covered hills and densely wooded canyons. At each turn there is a new view of Point Sur, 15 miles to the north.

The road levels out about four miles up as it passes several homes, remote nests for people who have no need of neighbors. Looking down from an outcropping near the top, the trail seems like a snake twisting away to shaded canyons. Near the few homes at the ridge top, the Terrace Creek trail branches. This trail drops about a mile and a half, through grass and oak, down to redwoods and the terraced creek

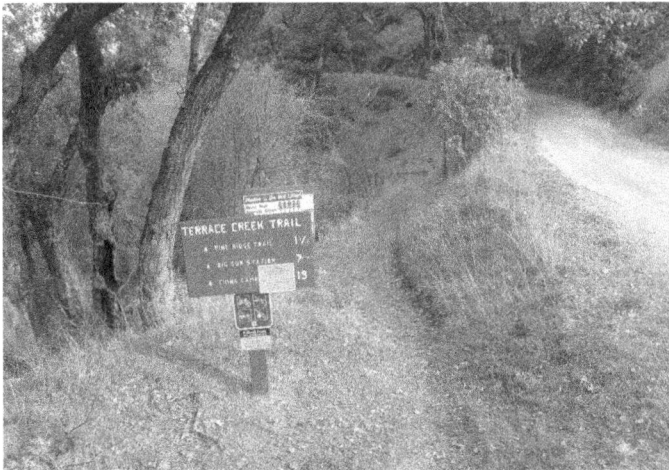

that gives the trail its name. Terrace Creek trail ends at the Pine Ridge Trail, and an alternate hike would be down Terrace Creek to the trail camp and north five more miles to the Forest Service parking lot.

To do this alternate hike, a car would be left at the Forest Service parking lot, about two miles north of the Ventana Inn. This hike would be about 10 to 11 miles.

While the side trip down Terrace Creek is well worth the extra effort, the Coast Ridge Road continues on, with views that just seem to get better. There is another side road leading to another, even more remote home. Soon there is another gate, the end of human habitat. Beyond the gate, there is the Ventana wilderness to the left and a vertical drop to the Pacific Ocean to the right.

From the gate to Timber Top is about two more miles. Along the way, there is grove of some of the largest madrones I've ever seen. The shade of these trees makes a good place to stop for lunch and a magnificent view. An alternative lunch stop is at the campground at Timber top, another mile south.

Timber Top is a small peak, and the Coast Ridge Road bends inland to go around it, so if the hiker finds herself away from the coastal view and dropping behind a small mountain, she has missed the exit.

Before arriving at Timber Top, a dirt bank rises up, blocking the view of the ocean. A side trail exits up and over that bank. Then it turns into a single track trail that drops along the side of the hill for a few dozen yards before coming to the trail camp and old stock pens at Timber Top. There is an old water tank there and other signs of days when someone ran cattle on the ridge. It's worth exploring, and the hike a few yards to the top offers even finer views.

Below the camp and old pens, the trail, now widening out to something close to a jeep track, runs out along a westward ridge before dropping out of sight. This is the start of Borronda Ridge, an old fire road that drops about two and a half to three miles to Highway One. From this point on the hiker has to consciously remind himself to watch where he's going, as the views are breathtaking making it hard for him to look away.

It is literally all downhill from here. The trail drops almost 3,000 feet in under three miles. The trail is easy to follow, and when in doubt, head downward. With the exception of a small clump of trees, the entire route is grass and small shrubs, allowing views of almost the entire Big Sur coast at every footfall.

If taking this hike in early spring, the wildflowers along the way are rich and spectacular, and on the roadway, where there is little vegetation, tiny beautiful flowers have found their niche. These are what a friend's grand kids call belly flowers, meaning you have to get down on your belly to really see them. I recommend being a kid again and actually doing that.

During the summer, the hiker will go from clear, sunny skies to fog right about 2,000 feet elevation, but the rest of the year it is clear top to bottom. At about this point there is a rock outcropping just off the trail, where the hiker can look straight down. It was there I once watched a small group of deer, unaware of me almost directly above.

About half way down the grassland gives way to coastal chaparral.

Shortly before the bottom, the trail passes under the power lines, and there is a road off to the left that leads to private property, but the main trail continues down toward the highway and ocean until arriving at the bottom at the old stock pens where at one time people must have loaded cattle into trucks. Then, a ten to fifteen minute shuttle back to Ventana Inn and perhaps an expensive lunch.

This is definitely a hike that begs for a camera, no matter what time of year.

Getting there. The Ventana Inn is on State Highway One, about 28 miles south of the last signal in Carmel (Rio Road). After passing Pfeiffer Big Sur State Park, the highway climbs, and the Ventana Inn is a left turn at the top of the hill. The parking area at Borronda Ridge is approximately 5 miles south, 500 yards south of the Coast Gallery.

5 Fort Ord Public Lands: a haven for wanderers (May/June 2010)

Looking up from the almost new parking lot, I remembered first seeing Fort Ord, on Monterey Bay, in the 1960s, where, as a member of the National Guard, I was sent for basic training. At the time I was not impressed.

With most military facilities close to Highway One, this fairly remote eastern part of the fort was wide open, and the only time I saw it was on the twenty mile march and overnight camp out. However, wearing ill-fitting, blister-promoting boots and carrying an equally ill-fitting pack and heavy rifle, as I marched in a line, also did not impress me. I remember sandy roads and shrubs, along with damp, chilly weather.

Fast forward several decades, and the military has only a small presence, there is a major state university, some housing developments, a shopping center and loads of public open space. Now, I make a special trip to hike there.

After Fort Ord closed in1994, redevelopment took over. Twenty percent of the fort is now developed, and eventually it will be no more than forty percent, leaving sixty percent for hiking, biking and horseback riding. That means over 83 miles of trails take you through 7,200 acres of pleasant valleys, rounded

hills, and high sandstone ridges with great views of the Salinas
Valley, Monterey Bay and the Ventana range.

There are several access points and gates of entry for hikers on this BLM-run land. There are also places to park inside the
old fort, with popular places for walkers, joggers, bikers and dog
owners. While these areas are forested and contain ponds, they're
places that once saw daily military activity. Also, there are some
closed areas due to unexploded ordinance.

However, my favorite spot is the eastern corner (Creek-
side Terrace), not heavily used even during the fort's military
heyday. Think of Fort Ord as a big triangle. One side is Highway
One, containing most of the development, another is Reservation
Road, through Marina, and the third is Highway 68, connecting
Monterey and Salinas. I prefer to start hiking near where Reservation and Highway 68 meet.

Standing in the parking area off Reservation Rd., which
runs along the bottom of the Fort Ord hills, at the edge of the
Salinas River flood plain, I can see several trails and pick the
start of my hike. To the right a paved road and a trail (#30) rise
steeply to a ridge, covered with scrub and dropping abruptly in
sandstone bluffs, complete with small caves and colorful outcroppings of rock. Another, greener ridge rises to the left, with a
trail (#01) wrapping around the end of the bluff before climbing
to the ridge. Ahead, off the gated, paved road a few yards past
the horse trailer parking is trail #31. It rises through grassy oak
woodland to a saddle. Beyond that saddle is a bowl, lush and
green in the spring and honeycombed with intersecting trails.

This is not the place for someone who hikes to a destination. The trails are remnants of the jeep and tank roads and
marching trails from the military days, so trails constantly cross
and interconnect. The idea is to just take off, hit a junction and
pick a direction and continue making choices until you either
find yourself looking back down on the parking area or decide to
retrace you steps. Sometimes you choose between a well worn,
well-marked trail and one, half grown over, that just goes off into
the trees.

Walk a few yards up the road to trail (#31), which leads

off to the left. It winds through oak, brush and high grasses for about three quarters of a mile to the saddle. From there, you can go left to the southern ridge, right (#34) to get a close look at sandstone bluffs and caves before a quick, steep climb to the northern ridge or take one of the two trails down into the forested bowl.

At the western end of the bowl, about another mile, trail 32 rises again, before ending at Engineer Canyon Rd. A short walk to the left will connect with trail 35 or 39. Another section of rolling hills has a network of trails, leading to Jack's Road and another group of trails and so on throughout the fort.

Or, starting from the lot, take the dirt trail heading right to a ridge with views of the Salinas Valley. This trail meets a dirt road running along the ridge that con-

tinues for miles. That dirt road follows the top of the sandstone bluffs and intersects the steep (#34) trail. Further on another steep trail (#32) drops you to the western end of the bowl.

The left trail (#01) winds around the ridge and climbs quickly to where you can look back down on the parking area or south over Highway 68 to Jack's Peak Regional Park and the Ventana. You can continue along this ridge until you find a trail that drops you back into the bowl or down to the dirt road that leads along 68 toward Laguna Seca raceway and another group of trails (#40,41,45,46,47 and 48).

There are about nine areas with networks of trails, all connected, and if you go straight in any direction, there is a road between these areas within about a mile, giving you points of reference along with a fairly direct route back to a trail head.

The ridges allow you to walk in a natural area while looking down at some of the richest farm land in the state and to the city of Salinas. However, once you drop down from the ridge, you feel like you could be a hundred miles from civilization.

In just a few miles you can wander from grassy hills to coastal shrub-land, all strewn with coast live oaks. This high ground was formed from ancient dunes, which are still sand in some places, sandstone in others. The abrupt drop down to Reservation Road marks the edge of the Salinas Valley, with its rich farms.

As I walked along the southern ridge, I noticed clumps of native bunch grass, reminding me how relatively pristine this area, surrounded by Monterey Bay cities, has managed to remain.

If your timing is right and you are lucky, you might catch sight of black tailed deer, turkeys, bobcats, coyotes, badgers, red tailed hawks, Canadian geese, California quail, gopher snakes, coast horned lizards, golden eagles, and mountain lions.

Another access point is from highway 68, on Toro Creek Rd., in a small housing development across from Toro Regional Park. You can also access the western part of the fort by exiting Hwy. 1 at Lightfighter and take the first right (1st). Then turn left on Gigling Rd. and drive to the parking area at the corner of 8th. Motorized traffic is prohibited beyond this point. Walk east on Gigling and turn left into the oak forest at any trail that looks tempting. Then just wander through the maze of trails until you discover one of the ponds. It was somewhere in this maze of trails and occasional ponds where I flushed groups of wild turkeys one spring day.

Shade is somewhat sparse, particularly in the upper areas, and it can be hot and dusty on a summer afternoon on the higher ridges. However, no matter how convoluted your wanderings, you are never far from civilization.

The trails range from wide, dirt roads used by bikes, single track trails to trails that look seldom used and have sprouted small wildflowers. some trails have posts with trail numbers, and others and not marked. Not all the trails are on the map, but it's almost impossible to get lost. Do bring a map and water. A good map can be found at (http://www.blm.gov/pgdata/etc/medialib/blm/ca/pdf/hollister.Par .64029.File.dat/current_version_trail_map.pdf). You can get more trail into at 831-394-8314. More information is also available at http://www.blm.gov/ca/st/en/fo/hollister/fort_ord/index.html.

Portola drive exits Reservation Road just before it intersects with Highway 68. You can see the parking lot on the right from Reservation Rd.

Heading back to the coast on Reservation, entering Marina, Wild Tyme Coffee and deli is in a business park on the right. Further up there are all the normal fast food places. Taking 68 to Salinas and Highway 101 takes you past many places to eat and drink.

Getting There
Fort Ord Public Lands

    From Htghway 101, take the John St, (Highway 68) exit in Salinas toward Monterey (right going south, left going north). At the intenection of John and S. Main, Higway 68 continues on S. Main (left turn), to the intersection of River Rd./Reservation Rd. Go right on Reservation, a very short way, to the first left (Portola). At the fork (Creekside Terrace Road), go right to Fort Ord open space parking.

    From Highway 1 at the town of Marina, take Reservatio Road east about 9 miles to Portola Road, just before the intersection with Highway 68. Turn right and go right agaln at fork (Creekside Terrace Road) to parking.

6 Urban Wilderness (Redwood Regional Park July/Aug. 2010)

I lived in the San Francisco Bay area for several years and hiked many places, mostly on the peninsula, but I recently got a pleasant surprise, a huge, popular spot unknown to me.

An email from California Wilderness Coalition advertised a hike in the Oakland Hills at Redwood Regional Park. Since I am always curious about new places, and I know what a good group Cal Wild is, I made the 80 mile drive.

Approaching the park, I could look down at downtown Oakland, San Francisco and Alameda, just a few miles away.

This 1,829 acre park is bordered by an affluent neighborhood, with some homes actually backing up to the park. There are several trailheads off of Skyline Blvd.: Canyon Meadows Staging Area, MacDonald Gate Staging Area, Big Bear Gate, Roberts Rec. Area, Redwood Bowl Staging Area, Moon Gate and Skyline Gate Staging Area, the jumping off place for my hike. And there is even an equestrian area.

The first thing I noticed from the parking lot was that while it was late May, everything as far as I could see was richly green. Lines of trees dropped away to a distant, unseen reservoir. At a time of year when much of California is turning brown, this area still shouts spring time.

We started off on the West Ridge Trail, a wide dirt road that also doubles as the first leg of the bike trail that rings the park. This trail undulates along the high side of the park, and it sports a lush mixed forest of redwood groves, other evergreens, including some beautiful twisted madrones and deciduous trees.

It's a popular trail, an easy walk for families out for a stroll.

After a little over a mile, we turned off at the Tres Sendas trail, a no bike hiking trail. The Tres Sendas dropped steeply, over rocks, tree roots and stream crossings, requiring close attention to where we put our feet. Soon we had left the open skies for the dense redwood forest. The trail followed a tiny stream that feeds Redwood Creek, which in turn is a tributary of San Leandro Creek, which flows down to Upper San Leandro Res.

On the way down, we crossed the French Trail, which goes both back up to the West Ridge and also deeper into the park. At the bottom of the hill, we hit Redwood Creek and turned left. In a few yards we came to a wide spot with benches and a fence along the creek. There was a sign saying that stream and bank restoration was underway. The sign featured pictures of rainbow trout and Calif. newt, two of the area's endangered species.

The park officials were trying to eliminate the erosion caused by extensive foot traffic, erosion that fouls the stream bottom and adversely affects the spawning pools.

Along the stream was a true redwood forest, with ferns and very few other types of trees. Splashes of sunlight alternated with deep shade.

At this point we could have followed the Stream Trail south for perhaps two and a half miles along the stream to Redwood Gate at the southern end of the park, but we were on a guided hike, so we turned north and started heading up the hill.

Soon the forest changed, becoming a mixed forest and

then a deciduous forest. The canopy opened up again, and we reached for our sun glasses.

About half way up the trail, we ran into Girls Camp. It was located in a grassy meadow, with a fire ring, some picnic benches and a restroom. We stopped there for lunch in the sunshine, wondering if anyone could camp there or only girl groups, perhaps scouts. While there are several picnic areas in the park, Girls Camp seems the only place to camp.

It was at the camp, while enjoying our snacks under puffy clouds and a gentle spring sun, that Julia, our leader, asked us to sign petitions for the desert protection act, which would establish new wilderness areas and less off road use in California's deserts. I was happy to sign. California Wilderness Coaliti has done so much to protect the lands in which I love to hike. To learn more about the organization, go to www.calwild.org.

After lunch, a short uphill trek took us back to the parking area, with restrooms and water, to Skyline Gate. From the parking area, East Ridge Trail goes off in the opposite direction from West Ridge, the other end of the bike loop. A short hike along this trail takes one to a trail into Huckleberry and Sibley Regional preservers. A short hike into Huckleberry leads to a bay forest, and Sibley has longer trails, including one to 1,763 foot Round Top, an ancient volcano and the highest point in the preserve. The park also abuts Anthony Chabot Regional Park to the south. There is access to the 31-mile East Bay Skyline National Recreation Trail, part of the Bay Area Ridge Trail system. In short, you can just keep walking as far as you wish.

It is also possible to follow the stream down to Upper San

Leandro Res. and continue on up to Las Trampas Regional
Wilderness, four or five miles to the east.

There are many species of wildlife in the park and adjoining preserves, including mountain lions and bobcats, deer, rac-
coons, rabbits, and squirrels. There are several kinds of snakes,
including rattlers, gopher snakes and striped racers. It is even
possible to catch sight of a rare golden eagle. However, if you
hope to view wildlife, pick a week day and go early, as the park,
located almost directly above downtown Oakland is popular with
east bay hikers.

While there is only one bike loop, there are many trails
for horses and dogs. It is a true multi use park, and from the lack
of trash, I assume a very well loved and respected park. It is also
a busy park. I can't recall seeing so many people on a trail. In
fact, two of the people on the hike said they jog there several
times a week.

*Getting there: From the south take the 880 to the 238 a
short way to 580 north. Take CA 13 to Joaquin Miller Rd. and go
right (up the hill) to Skyline. Turn left and follow Skyline. You'll
see parking areas and trail heads along the way. Skyline gate
holds the most cars. From the east: Take 680 to the 24, and go
west to CA13 to Joaquin Miller Rd. and follow directions above.
From the north or west: Take 580/80 to 24 east, to CA13 to
Joaquin Miller Rd. and continue as above. CA 13 is a short freeway connecting the 580 with the 24.*

7. Aerobic Vistas (Rocky Ridge, Sept./Oct. 2010)

When I want a really good, almost painful, aerobic workout, along with stunning views, I take one of the most popular hikes on the Big Sur Coast, Rocky Ridge. No matter the time of year or the weather, I'm never alone.

Just seven miles south of the last signal in Carmel (Rio Rd.) this hike is handy to the Monterey Peninsula and even Silicon Valley.

There are always cars on both sides of the highway, and once you park, look up, and if you don't get a crick in your neck, you'll be looking at Rocky Ridge. You can pick out the trail going up the ridge, and usually, if you have sharp eyes, you'll see someone hiking.

Actually, there are two ways to get up there. As you face inland, there is a trail on the right that leads into the canyon and follows Soberanes Creek. This is a popular way to make a loop out of the hike. However, if you are making a loop, do it from this direction, as there is a section most people don't want to descend.

Following the trail up the canyon leads over a bridge and through a short forest of cactus, which is rather surprising on the Big Sur coast. Soon the cactus gives way to shrubs before entering into a redwood forest along the creek. After about three miles, the trail rises up and suddenly makes a left turn out of the

forest. The next section is the part no one wants to descend. The next half mile feels and looks straight up, iit is an exercise in watching where you plant your boot.

This trail tops out in a little saddle between two small hill tops, where it meets the other, my preferred trail.

Starting back on the highway, the left trail, a few dozen yards north of the canyon, starts up from the highway and winds fairly steeply through some chaparral. If you do this hike from Feb through May, you'll be assaulted by a lush palette of wildflowers, such as bush lupine, morning glories, indian paint brush and sticky monkey flower.

The trail soon bends around the end of the ridge, just above that grove of cactus, and there it turns north and becomes quite steep. From this point on the trail follows the ridge line.

After a short, fairly bare stretch, where the loose crumbly trail requires keeping an eye on the ground, the flowers start up again. In a good spring, both sides of the trail are flooded with every color in the rainbow.

After a bit, you realize that this is a narrow ridge, the coast on the left and the steep hillside falling away to the canyon on the right. Down to the left is one of the most scenic sections of the Big Sur coast, with rock islands, Soberanes Point and rugged cliffs that drop away to an angry sea. Ahead, the trail just keeps climbing.

There are places where short trails lead off to the right. Walk the few feet, and you will look down at a steep-sided bowl that is the Soberanes Creek drainage. To the left is the top of the ridge, the grass and chaparral covered area accessed by the trail. Below is the dense redwood forest. Just ahead is that steep section reached from Soberanes Canyon.

After about two miles and about 1800 feet, a trail on the left leads a few yards to a bench perched on a clump of rock. Everyone stops there, both to catch their breath and to take in the view. Many locals, out for their daily or weekly aerobic hike, stop there, before turning back. The bench is almost directly above Highway One, and it gives a commanding view of miles of coast, from Point Lobos to Big Sur Coast. This is a place to linger and to thank your lucky stars you don't live in Kansas or Oklahoma.

From the bench, the top is a short hike, perhaps another half mile of steep ridge trail, again awash with flowers in the spring. When you turn away from the coast, you are pretty much at the top.

The trail follows around the north side of those two little hillocks, connecting with the trail out of the canyon and continuing inland for another mile before hitting the remnants of an old fence. Beyond the fence was once private land and off limits, but the Big Sur Land Trust bought the land, which connects to other public lands. There is no reason to stop. However, there aren't really defined trails, so it's best to pay attention to where you are. It is possible to connect with a dirt road that will take you back to Carmel or into Mittledorf Preserve miles inland. It is even possible to bushwhack around and down into the end of the canyon, but there is no trail, and it's not easy going.

However, those little hillocks at the top of the ridge are worth hiking. There are rock outcroppings there where you can sit and look back toward Carmel and down into Mal Paso

Canyon, the last residential road in Carmel Highlands. There are usually clusters of flowers growing around the rocks, and the views are incredible.

There is a lot to explore along the top, and since you pay a high energy price to get there, linger, explore, maybe even stretch out in a hollow out of the ocean breeze. Take in the buzz of insects and the smell of the blossoms.

I recommend going back down the ridge. If you opt to descend into the canyon, be careful. It is much steeper than the ridge. Also, going back down the ridge gives you views you do not get going up the canyon.

Once back to the highway, take a few minutes to cross to the ocean side and follow the trail south to Soberanes Point. Climb down the rocks to the rock and gravel beach for some tide pooling. Continue south on the trail and wrap around up the hill just above the point. It's call Whale Peak for a very good reason, and the short hike up during the migration months (winter/early spring and early summer) might reward you with the sight of migrating whales.

Walking down the north side of Whale Peak will connect you with the trail back to the parking area.

Getting there: The trail heads are almost exactly 7 miles south of the signal at Rio road, on Highway One, between mile post 65 and 66. There is a dirt pull off on both sides of the road, and the inland side, where the canyon trail starts, has a row of trees and an old shack.

8 Accessible Wilderness (Sonol Regional Wilderness, Nov./Dec. 2010)

The Sunol Regional Wilderness is just a short freeway drive from any Bay Area city, but it can make you feel you've stepped back to a time before the freeways and suburbs, to the days of vast ranches and unspoiled wetlands. This beautiful, scenic and rambling area is a short drive off the 680 freeway between Pleasanton and Fremont. The 6,858 acre wilderness encompasses bare peaks, wildflower strewn hills, oak woodlands, thick forests and a scenic gorge called Little Yosemite.

My recent exploration was on the Maguire Peak Trail, an eight mile loop with stunning views. The trail head is on Welch Creek Rd. off Calaveras Rd. However, before parking, you first have to continue a couple miles further on Calaveras Rd. to Geary Rd. to the main entrance to purchase the $5 parking permit.

The trailhead with a locked gate and places for very few cars is on the left, at about mile post 1.7. Another access, also on the left at mp .72, and a bit shorter, is Lower Maguire Peaks Trail, but we opted for the other.

The trail, an old dirt road left over from the ranching days, starts up steeply through oaks and grasslands and levels out near the rusting remains of some old ranch machinery and continues to climb again for about a mile, before starting down once

more. At the high point there are views of the valley along Calaveras Rd., the Alameda Creek valley and also of Maquire Peak, with its rocky outcroppings at the top, and of the trail running along the shoulder of the peak, the trail we were following.

As the trail drops, it enters a wooded area, passes a metal watering trough, like a giant bathtub on the hillside, just below the trail. At the bottom of the hill, in a clump of trees, the trail splits. This is the start of the loop portion that circumnavigates the peak. We turned left.

The trail rises steadily, dropping occasionally, along the southwest, dry, grassy side of the peak, and after a mile or more, rises above the hills to the west, affording some great views of Mt. Tamalpais, the distinctive peak in Marin County, many miles to the west. A little further on, and somewhat higher, the view starts to include San Francisco Bay and the dim outline of Richmond.

As the trail rounds the north end of the peak and starts to turn east, it rises very steeply for a short stretch to the high point on the loop, at over 1200 ft. elevation. There is a bench just off the trail, and from there I could see both Mt. Tamalpais and Mt. Diablo, the highest peak in the East Bay, at the same time. To the right and about 1,000 feet below was San Antonio Reservoir. The sweeping view extended from Marin County, to the San Francisco Bay and the East Bay to the Livermore Valley.

Behind the bench was the ridge leading up to the peak, 400 feet higher, and it looked like there might be a trail for a side trip to the top. Although no official trail is indicated on the map, it did look like a fairly easy steady climb up the ridge to the top.

Leaving the top and the bench, we dropped down to the northeast side of Maquire Peak, and there, on the more sheltered side, were great displays of wildflowers, including poppies, lupine, mustard, goldfield, owls clover and Indian paint brush. Also, as the trail dropped, we saw alder.

Madrone, willow, sycamore and pine abound. While the grasses on the other side was dry, this side was still green, a re-

sult of the last spring rains. The slope of the peak drops away to a valley, and the other side rises up to another trail that apparently leads to the wilderness boundary.

Rounding the bottom of the trail, we came again to where the loop branches. At the branch, unnoticed earlier in the day, we found a small pond or large mud hole, just off the junction.

We also noticed occasional side trails, probably leading to a view point, that had I not been with a group, I might have explored.

As we started up the last steep uphill, we encountered a group of cows on the trail. They made for the higher hillside as we approached. Cows in a wilderness seem out of place, but this was all once ranch land, and under the East Bay Regional Park District's multi-use land management policy, cattle continue to graze here.

Cattle were not the only non hikers we saw. This is a multi-use trail, so we encountered a group of very winded bicyclists, one walking his bike, a few equestrians and a local couple walking their dogs.

We picked up the pace on the final downhill stretch to the

cars, walking past beautiful old oak trees, patches of wildflowers and spring grasses. All agreed that it was an exceptional half day hike.

Once there, another must see, one I missed that day but sampled on another trip, is Little Yosemite on Alameda Creek. The name seems hard to believe until it is seen. To access this area, go back to the main entrance on Geary Rd. and park. The gorge is about two miles up the creek, and you can get there by walking up Ohlone Rd., which follows Alameda Creek, or take the more scenic McCorkle Trail through the hills, above the creek, and drop back down on Backpacking Rd. to the creek. And, yes, it does remind one of Yosemite and is well worth the extra walk to see the creek make its way through and around giant granite boulders.

When you pay for parking, you can get a map of the area, making it easy to find the trail and trailhead you want. Additionally, the trails are all in good condition and easy to follow and for the most part, well marked. you can concentrate on enjoying the views, rather than figuring out where you are. This wilderness is typical of the rolling oak woodland that people associate with central California.

Getting there: From the north (Hwy 80 or 580) take 680 south to the Calaveras Rd./Hwy 84 exit and go left on Calaveras Rd. four miles to Geary Rd., which leads into the park. Then to go to the Maquire Peak trailhead, go back Geary to Calaveras and back a short ways to Welch Creek Rd. on the right.
From the south (San Jose area), take 680 north to Calaveras Rd. and go right to the park, as per above.

9. Long Ridge: High Above the High Tech (Jan./Feb. 2011)

About ten miles as the crow flies from the heart of the silicon valley, the high tech hub, there is a string of open spaces and parks that make you feel like you're in another land at another time. Highway 35, also called Skyline Drive, stretches along the spine of the low mountains that separate the Santa Clara Valley from Santa Cruz and the San Mateo coast. From Castle Rock State Park, at the junction of the 35 and Highway 9 to the mountain community of Woodside, there is an almost continual string of open space preservers with names like Montebello, Los Trancos, Russian Ridge, Coal Creek, Skyline, Saratoga Gap and Long Ridge. There are also several state and city parks interwoven between them.

Highways 35 and 9 are popular with motorcycles, and the old dirt roads and trails that follow the highway are popular with bicycles, equestrians and hikers. Some trails are multi-use and others are reserved just for hikers. One can park at any trail head and just take off, and most of the trail heads have a kiosk with maps, making it easy to plan a trip that fits the mood and the available time.

Besides the easy access from populated areas, these open areas provide a delightful sampler of what's best about central California, that special mix of rolling grassland hills, studded with oaks, and mixed forests. The Long Ridge area offers a particularly rich and varied assortment of the local natural beauty. All in about a five mile loop. There are connecting trails that could keep one hiking for days.

Halloween turned to clear and sunny, just after a local rain, so hiking buddy Don and I pulled up to the Grizzly Flat trail head, about four miles north of the Hwy. 9 junction. Grizzly Flat, on the east side, is mostly grassy hilltops, so we opted to cross 35 and start down the spur to Long Ridge, and we soon discovered that we'd made the right choice.

After four tenths of a mile we hit the intersection of the Bay Area Ridge Trail, which follows Hwy. 35 for miles, and just beyond the junction we crossed a wooden bridge over almost dry Peters Creek. Just past the bridge the very steep end of Long Ridge went up to the right, and the Peters Creek Trail went left through a deep, mixed forest, cool and darkIt was a trail we could not resist.

In fall, Peters Creek only has water is certain spots, mostly standing, but with the winter rains it should be cascading over the rocks and logs before long. In the damp shade along the creek, rocks and trees were blanketed in mosses and lichens.

This mixed forest is primarily madrone, oak, bay laurel and buckeye, with some evergreen stands. The dense redwood forests being further to the west in Portola and Big Basin State parks. the smell of the bay laurel was at times intoxicating, along with the smell of damp earth.

We passed another route to Long Ridge, but kept going to the end of Peters Creek Trail. A pond is on private property, and there's a gate just to the left. Ducks swam lazily along, and reeds grew up along the bank. There the trail turned sharply to the right and climbed in switchbacks for a half mile before coming to Long Ridge. It is an old dirt road and undulates along the ridge. Looking west over a deep valley, we could see the coastal redwood parks and the distant ocean. At the junction Ward Road. descends west, eventually connecting with the trails of Portola State Park. We walked it a short way to see where it went, but it started to drop steeply, so we turned back.

Back on Long ridge, we found a side trail that went a few yards to an overlook, where we sat down among the rocks and had lunch.Up on Long Ridge, there are private parcels scattered among and between the open spaces. There were also either deer or stock trails cutting across the grassy hills.

After a few minutes the road ended, and a bench sat on the edge of the hill, offering a panoramic view of the coastal mountains. Past the bench the road ended at private property, and Long Ridge, slightly to the right, again became a single track trail, dropping from the open grassland hills back into the forest.

The dappled afternoon light played among the trees as we descended. And all long our hike we encountered mountain bikers, all moving fairly slowly and being quite courteous, which we found delightful.

After another half mile, we discovered one reason for the bikers' good behavior. At the next junction, where Long Ridge goes in two directions to reconnect with Peters Creek, there were two country rangers, one holding something that looked like a police radar gun, and apparently it was. They were clocking the bikers on their descent and giving tickets to speeders and reckless riders.

After a pleasant exchange and advice on which route was best, we headed down the less steep trail to the right, intersecting after a half mile with Peters' Creek. From there we retraced our steps back toward the trail head, stopping to check a short trail that lead to a solitary tree. Taking a second look we saw that it was an apple tree with some fruit sill hanging, so we stopped to pick an apple snack.

We talked about meeting the rangers and how nice it is to be in a park area that has the funds to keep several rangers on duty. Neighboring Castle Rock State Park has only one ranger for the entire property.

As we crossed the creek on the bridge, we started up the final four tenths of a mile to the car. Going back up hill and out of the trees, we realized that it had turned into a lovely, warm fall day. We had walked just shy of five miles. We passed the last junction below the road and watched the Bay Area Ridge Trail undulating along the sunlit hillside, bound for Woodside. We knew we'd only touched a small sample of the area and vowed to return again soon and tackle another of the dozens of trails to be had.

We were impressed by the peace and silence along the way, with a busy highway near by and the entire Santa Clara Valley a few miles down the hill. Yes, we thought, you really can get away, without actually getting away.

Getting there: Take Highway 9 either from the Saratoga/Los Gatos area in Santa Clara County or from Santa Cruz/San Lorenzo Valley. Highway 9 crosses Highway 35 at the top of the ridge that separates the coast from Silicon Valley. Go north four miles to the trailhead, easily spotted on the right.

10. Montera Mountain and Brooks Falls (March/Apr. 2011)

It had been well over twenty years since I last hiked up to Montera Mountain, when I lived in Pacifica and hiked all over the local hills. At the time, a recently retired gentleman started building a trail out of San Pedro Valley County Park to the Montera Mountain trail. Before that, we had to hike up into the east side of the park and bushwhack up to the San Francisco Fish and Game Refuge along Sweeny Ridge. Then we took the fire road to the mountain. That was the San Francisco watershed, and I believe we should have had permits to hike there.

Having last hiked it in the late 80s, it was a treat to return. The Montera Mountain trail starts next to the restroom, off the parking lot. There's a visitor's center a few yards away, but it's only open on weekends.

The trail is excellent, and wide enough for two to easily walk abreast. It zigzags up the side of the hill, through the chaparral, offering views of more and more of Pacifica at each turn. Then it enters the eucalyptus forest, something the park people tried to eradicate in the 80s. The forest thinned somewhat, but eventually, the project was dropped.

In the spring, you'd be greeted with an assortment of wildflowers. My winter trip was without anything in bloom, but the lower trail was lined with monkey flower, which should be brilliant yellow by early March.

There is wildlife along the trail. I saw mostly lizards, cottontail rabbits and lots of birds, but if you hike near either sunrise or sunset, you might catch sight of a bobcat or even a mountain lion.

It's a well-designed trail, with a continual, moderate, comfortable grade with lots of switchbacks and occasional benches where the views are the best, and offer good photo opportunities. Then, at about 1.1 miles, there's a well signed fork, with the left being the Brooks Falls Trail. This is best saved for the return trip.

About a half mile further, the trail abruptly changes to a narrow, rocky single track. This is where the sedimentary rocks meet granite. Tectonic forces have brought at least three different rock formations together at Montera Mountain. I found it instructive to pause and see this geological divide. As the trail changes, the rolling land suddenly gives way to rock walls, and the trail winds up the wall. It's the same rock face that causes Brooks Falls.

The rocky trail gave way further up to a very deeply rutted trail, where the rains and hikers have cut a deep grove. It's a good place to have poles, which I remembered to bring, as there are places where it's one foot in front of the other. There is a pair of signs along this stretch. Going up, the sign says entering McNee Ranch Park. Going down, it says entering San Pedro Valley Park.

At about 2.4 miles, this narrow trail ends at the fire road. Going right would take you down to Highway One at Montera Beach, a steep fire road. Going left is the last leg of the hike. Along this stretch, there are almost continual views to the south of Pacifica, Daly City, parts of San Francisco and the hills of Marin County. The rock wall on the north is dotted with ferns and lichens.

Along this fire road, cut out of rock, are the only two steep places, short stretches that felt aerobic. Then the road turned slightly south, and a side trail heads off toward south peak. North Peak, which is slightly higher is along the main road and has transmitter towers on it.

I was almost to the top, when two women walked by me. They were walking and talking, and they

stopped just a couple of hundred years from the top. They turned around and started to descend..

A little over a mile on this fire road, there's a left turn at the base of the peak. There were a couple of trucks with men working when I arrived. Walking past where the trucks were parked, another short, maybe five yard path ends at the top. From up there, at almost 1900 feet, I had a clear view of northern San Francisco Bay, the airport, with the occasional plane rising over the hills, Oakland, San Francisco, Mount Diablo, (over 35 miles away) and Mt. Tamalpias in Marin County. Looking south, the coast twisted toward Half Moon Bay, and to the east, you can see the rolling hills of San Francisco Fish and Game Refuge, eventually dropping down to Crystal Springs Res., along Highway 280.

After taking some photos, I sat down on a rock next to the geologic survey marker and had a bit of lunch before starting down.

Coming down the short spur to the top, I looked eastward along the fire road. This can be followed a bit further until end ends at the watershed. There are miles of trails in the watershed, and if you are interested, check the internet for trails and access points. As far as alternative routes up to Montera Mountain, there is a trail/road at the end of Higgins Way, off Adobe Dr. in Pacifica, as well as the trailhead just south of Devil's slide at Montera Beach.

But those are other trips. This time, I retraced my steps to the junction and then down the trail to San Pedro Valley Park. On that badly eroded section, a trail runner went by me, a very sure footed fellow. When I got to the junction with the Brooks Falls Trail, I turned to another nicely maintained trail, first following a ridge through the chaparral, before turning right and heading down into a wooded area. The granite cliff face was off to my right, as I descended.. I found a bench and figured I was near the falls. I sat down and pulled out the camera. Unfortunately, the falls were in the shadows, and the sun was over the ridge and in my face. Photography was impossible.

The falls are some distance from the trail, and they're probably best seen in the spring, when the sun is higher. It's a long thin falls that drops down a steep cliff.

After leaving the bench, I entered a fairly dense mixed forest, with stands of Manzanita, various deciduous trees and eucalyptus. The trail drops down into a side canyon that feeds San Pedro Creek, and near the bottom, the trail meets the Old Trout Farm Trail, a nice side trip if you aren't anxious to get back. It's a short hike up the creek in a thick forest. However, if you continue down to the visitor's center, you're almost there.

Getting there: Take Highway One to the southern most signal in Pacifica, Linda Mar Blvd. Go up Linda Mar about two miles to the end (Oddstad Blvd.) and turn right. The entrance to the park is right there on the left. The parking fee is $5, and the park closes at 5PM.

11. Preview: Mt. Konocti (July/Aug. 2011)

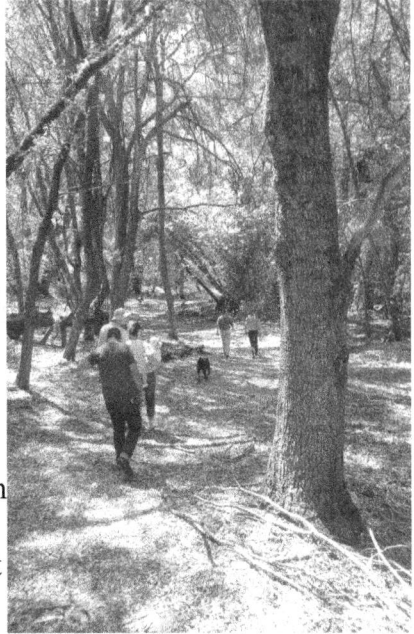

Sometimes a hike is not a hike, possibly a tour, a preview or even a scouting trip, but not something where boots spend much time on the ground. That was the case when I was among the first group of visitors to see Mt. Konocti, that group of five peaks that towers over Clear Lake at Kelseyville.

The Outdoor Writers Association of California, as part of their spring conference, were given an opportunity to get a pre-opening look at this soon to be public recreation area. Alan Flora, an associate planner for the County of Lake, led a small convoy of county vehicles to the top of Wright Peak, one of the five that comprise Konocti. He opened the locked gate at the start of the County's land, and we drove through, a benefit that will be denied to future hikers.

The Mt. Konocti area, scheduled to open to the public on August 27, will have a parking area and a restroom at the locked gate, with a stile for entry by other than motor vehicles. A quarter mile below the gate will be the main parking area, and a quarter mile further down the road will be an equestrian staging area. The trail, actually a dirt road, will be multi use.

The trail will climb steadily for three miles and a 2300 ft. elevation gain to the top of Wright Peak. A bit over a mile from the top a fork with a sign will lead about .7 miles to Buckingham Peak, and about .1 mile from the top of Wright Peak will be another fork, leading to Howard Peak. The ambitious hiker can stand atop three peaks, all approximately the same altitude, on a single day.

So, let us find out what you're going to experience. The scenery I saw eas mostly from the window of a jeep, through swirls of dust.

After you've driving the two miles of well-graded dirt road to the parking area, you'll hike through some brush and low trees to private land. This is why the delay until late summer. The existing road cuts through a walnut grove,and runs right by a farmer's home. The road/trail will be rerouted around the grove and away from the house. You'll know when you're back on county land again by the bench along the trail.

Soon you'll move into a mixed forest, dominated by live oak, pine and bay. After about a mile, you'll see the junction to Buckingham Peak, where there'll be a sign. You can hike almost to the topmost part of the peak, but since there's a communication tower site up there, you can't stand on the exact summit. But, since we did not go that way, I'll concentrate on Wright Peak.

About 3/4 of a mile further you'll see a sign and some amenities. I'm not exactly sure what the amenities are, but this is the junction to a short hike to Mary Downen's cabin, long abandoned. Standing at the cabin and looking to the left, over that low ridge, is supposedly the largest canyon live oak in North America. You can nott prove this by me, so you'll just have to bushwhack up there and see for yourself. Just past the cabin is an open field, formerly an orchard, and at the end of the field you'll find great views of Clear Lake.

A tenth of a mile further up the road is the second restroom and amenities, and this is where the trial makes a hard left. Another tenth of a mile and you'll find another bench. At this point, you start getting some views again, and .2 mile later is the fork to Howard Peak. You now have just over .1 mile to either peak.

The top of Wright Peak, at 4300 plus feet has an old California Department of Forestry fire lookout, complete with antennas and transmitters. It is unmanned, and unfortunately, it will be locked. We were with someone with the key, so we made the 71 steps to the top for a very windy 360 degree view of Lake County. You will have to walk around to various

view sites at the top to get these views piecemeal.

While standing at the top, we got a geology lesson from a local wine maker. Lake County is at the junction of the geologically unstable San Andreas Fault area and the equally unstable Cascade range, as in Mt. Lassen and Mt. Shasta. In fact, these peaks have seen volcanic eruptions as recently as 35,000 years ago. It is quite likely they will see more action in the future. In fact, when farmers were preparing their land for wine grapes, on a hillside property directly south of the summit, tons of obsidian, (a shiny, black, glass-like volcanic rock), had to be cleared.

There's even more odd geology. Possibly one of the largest caverns in the country is located under the mountain, but the entrances have either collapsed over the years or have been bulldozed closed for public safety. Apparently a couple of hundred years ago, during an extended drought, the local native Americans were able to enter the caverns from what is now under water.

From the top, looking south, you can see the lower lake and the patchwork of wineries.

The upper lake is to the north, and if you visit during winter or spring, you will see a snow-capped mountain in the distance. That mountain, at the north end of the county is, you guessed it, Mt. Snow. And if it is a very clear day, usually in the morning, you can look to the east for a glimpse of Sutter Buttes,

the small-
est moun-
tain range
in the
country.
To the
west the
mountains
continue
to undu-
late away
to Mendo-
cino
County.

With the exception of the short trail to the cabin and beyond, the existing trails are all dirt roads, which makes the hike
moderate to strenuous. Moderate because the road has a steady
grade, strenuous because it is a continual uphill for three miles.
Eventually, more hiking trails will be opened up, presumably
permitting access to all five peaks. So if you enjoy the hike and
decide to return the following year, there may be more to see. In
the mean time, there are places where it would not be hard to
bushwhack a bit for some further exploration. You can not be the
first group up there, but if you come on August 27, you could be
the second.

*To get there from the 101, come up either Hwy. 20 out of
Calpella or the 175 out of Hopland. From either direction, you'll
connect with Hwy 29. Then go south to Kelseyville, about fifteen
minutes south of Lakeport, and go one block past the signal at
Live Oak Dr. and turn left on Main St. Go a few short blocks to
Mt. Konocti Dr., at the high school, and turn right. In a few
blocks the paved road ends at the two mile dirt road to the parking area.*

*From the south, drive up Napa Valley to Calistoga and
continue up the 29 to Main in Kelseyville. From the east, take the
20, off I-5 at Williams and make the long drive to the 53, and then
go south to the 29 and up the west side of the lake to Main St.*

12. Where the High Tech Trek (Rancho San Antonio Park. Sept/Oct 2011)

Sandwiched between Los Altos Hills and Cupertino is a rich mixture of terrains, vegetation and scenery, along with miles of trails. It is so close to the Silicon Valley scene, that it takes only five minutes from trailhead to latte. This is Rancho San Antonio County Park and Open Space Preserve, just a mile off busy I-280.

Even during the week, this is a very popular place, and on weekends the foot traffic is reported to be almost congested. However, as in most trail systems, walk a mile and the crowd thins out to occasional other hikers.

The parking lot has nice restrooms and water fountains, kiosks and trail maps. We left the parking lot, crossed a short bridge and turned right on a gravel path, which was paralleled by a paved bike path. In 3 tenths of a mile we passed tennis courts, and exited the county park to enter the open space preserve. We took the Lower Meadow trail, still wide, populated and almost flat. After a half mile, we forked left on the Farm Bypass Trail, which took us to Dear Hollow Farm in .3 mile. It's a well preserved old still working farm, with a cow, pigs, goats, sheep, chickens, other animals. There is an organic garden as well as numerous turn-of-the-century ranch buildings. An additional attraction is the restored Grant Cabin, furnished to represent living conditions in the late 1800s.

A tractor from 1922 was displayed in the field beside the trail. Some people only strolled as far as the farm, stopping to look at the place, get the feel for an earlier, quieter time and perhaps feed or pet the goats.

Along the way, scattered on the side of a hill, a group of wild turkeys foraged for food. We also saw rabbits right off the trail, so used to people that they did not bother running from us.

We left the wide trails and buildings behind, as we started up the Rogue Valley Trail, which left the open meadows, strewn with a few trees and started into the forest. In another half mile we intersected with the Wildcat Loop Trail. We could have continued on Rogue Valley to the Chamise Trail to the Black Mountain Trail, some three miles further at the far end of the preserve, but there was no loop. We would have ended up far from the parking lot.

Instead, we started up the Wildcat Loop Trail, a fairly steep climb, with a series of switchbacks. We were now in the thick of the forest with Madrone, Bay, Oak, Big Leaf Maple, willow and Sycamore. Along the shaded side of the trail, sticky monkey flower and indian paint brush were still in bloom, even though it was late July. After .9 mile, we reached a grassy hill top, where four trails intersected. One of these went just .1 mile to a vista point. Squirrels were darting across the trail and up the trees at almost every turn.

We continued back into the woods on the Wildcat Loop Trail for .6 mile to the junction of the Upper Wildcat Canyon Trail. This trail that came down from the Upper High Meadow Trail a couple miles higher. Rather than go up, we went down the Wildcat Loop for .2 miles, found a deeply shaded grove of tall trees with some fallen logs and stopped for lunch.

Our lunch was at a trail junction, and the Wildcat Loop was only a half mile directly back to the farm. We were not ready

to call it a day. the other trail was the Pacific Gas & Electric (PG&E) trail, a 2.1 mile trek back to the car. This trail climbed very steeply at first, less so as we hit the wide road used by PG & E trucks. Steep trails after meals are not fun, but soon we were loosened up and climbing high above the county park. The trail peaks at almost 1000 feet, and up there, following PG & E's high tension power lines; we were treated to some incredible views of the Silicon Valley. Moffett Field was visible, where the huge hangers seemed almost directly below us, as was the Shoreline Amphitheatre, a major south bay concert venue. It was interesting to be in a vast open space and to be able to look down at a busy metropolitan area.

A large number of the trails are also equestrian trails, and the PG & E is one of those. We could see the impressions of horse shoes in the dirt, and at one point we passed a horse watering trough. There are a few hiking only trails, but all the bike trails are in the county park, within a half mile of the parking lot.

It seemed like we were never going to reach the top, and I wondered how steep the downhill would be when we finally got there. Then it started to drop until we were down again on a grassy hillside. Below us was a huge water tank, and when we got to it, the trail turned to the left.

Passing the tank, we could see the county park still well below us, and the trail dropped steeply until it ended at a road. It was only a short hike to the right until we picked up the gravel path again, which brought us back to the bridge and the parking lot. By then it was well after two in the afternoon and quite warm. The lot, almost full when we arrived, was over half empty.

People obviously preferred to hike in the cool of the morning.

Even up on the high trails, we passed other hikers and runners, but they were rather few, and we often had long stretches of trail to ourselves.

Well marked trails, a wide variety of terrain and view shed and the easy access from a major freeway, makes this a desirable place to hike. There is also a nice variety of wildlife, including the much advertised but not seen mountain lions. Our five and a half mile trek exposed us to about a quarter of the available 23 miles of trails, so we have every intention of returning soon.

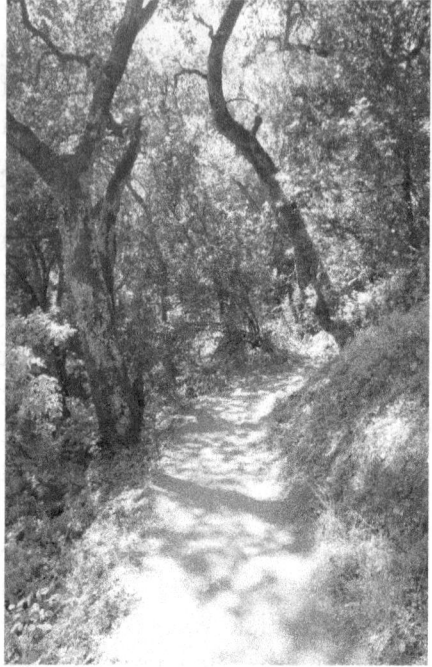

Getting there: From I-280, north or south, take the Foothill Boulevard exit and proceed south on Foothill Boulevard approximately 0.2-mile to Cristo Rey Drive. Turn right on Cristo Rey Drive, continue for about 1 mile, veer right around the traffic circle, and turn left into the County Park entrance. There are several parking lots, including one designated for equestrian trailers. The trailhead for the preserve is located adjacent to the 85-car parking area in the northwest lot.

13 Mill Creek Preserve: A truly pleasant hike (Nov/Dec 2011)

If you like redwood forests, good trails, lots of streams and waterfalls and an ocean view, you probably can't find a better hike than Mill Creek Redwood Preserve.

The Monterey Peninsula Regional Park District operates a diverse series of parks around the Carmel, Carmel Valley and Big Sur areas. Some, like Garland Ranch in Carmel Valley, are open to anyone at any time. Others, like Mill Creek, are open to the public via a permit process, permits being available on-line from 48 to 72 hours before the date you wish to hike. You can get information on Mill Creek, along with a link to the permit application at http://www.mprpd.org/index.cfm/id/25/Mill-Creek-Redwood-Preserve/.

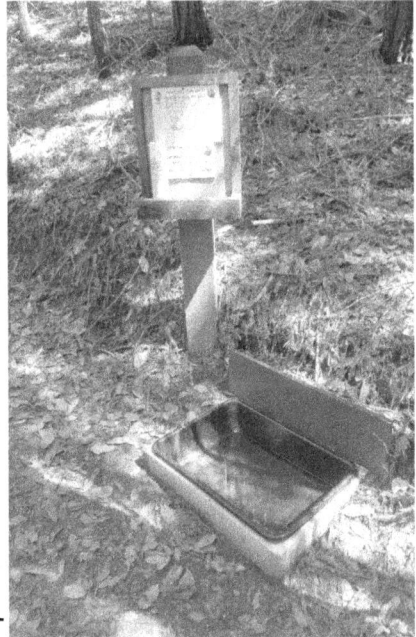

You can fill the application out on-line, and the permit will be e-mailed to you. There is limited parking at the trail head, so there are limited permits for any given day, and it would be good to have an alternate date, just in case.

As it says on the web site, there is only one trail, 2.75 miles in length, one-way. This moderate trail has only a 250 foot elevation change, so it's more of a very pleasant walk than an aerobic workout.

Mill Creek Redwood Preserve is 1,534 acres of very rugged Big Sur coastal redwood canyon land. The preserve, on a very steep slope, was pieced together from several large properties between 1988 and 2000 for costs totaling $2 million. The 5.5 mile out-and-back route was completed in 2006; taking 10 years to construct by hand. The craftsmanship, the park district claims, is reminiscent of the Civilian Conservation Corps era of trail building during the Great Depression. Personally, I'd be surprised if the CCC built trails of this quality. The trail is almost wide enough for two abreast in places and is flat, so keeping your footing is not a problem. In some places rock from along the trail has been broken up and used to create a bank. Near river crossings, interlocked beams hold the trail up, and the bridges, unlike the ones in the Indiana Jones films, are rock solid.

There is parking for perhaps 8 to 10 cars along Palo Colorado Road. The trail head sign is very small, so it's wise to check the odometer at the base of Palo Colorado Rd. and start looking when you pass mile six. The small sign is on the right.

Almost as soon as you drop down the trail, there's a place to disinfect your shoes to keep sudden oak death from infecting the forest. There's a can of Lysol and a shoe bath with 10 percent bleach. Please use this, as the local forests have been devastated in recent years.

Shortly after cleaning your shoes, you cross the first of several streams on one of those indestructible bridges. This creek, like the others in the preserve, are full in spring and slow as the summer and fall progress.

The trail rises slightly after the first bridge to the next bridge and much smaller stream. It pretty much levels out until the last three quarters of a mile, when it gradually climbs to the 1,986 feet high point at the end of the trail.

The trail, which follows the contour of the steep hillside, runs through a mixed forest of redwoods, madrone, oak and bay. As the trail undulates along the hillside, it seems to cross a stream about every third to half mile. One of these, at least in spring when I hiked it, was flowing fast and hard, with small waterfalls above the trail and one fairly long one below. When we stopped to check out the lower fall, we realized that the water was running, as if on a rock face, down a redwood that had fallen in the water way.

As we continued, we saw some rock formations along the trail, places where water brought minerals into the cracks in the rock, where they'd crystallized in swirling patterns. In other places, thick blankets of lichen covered the rocks and the shady sides of the trees.

Along the way, we heard woodpeckers tapping, unseen, in the forest around us. We heard the occasional call of an owl. A cat-sized animal dashed off the trail and into the woods before we could get a good look to identify it.

For most of the hike, the dappled sunlight splattered on the ground between the trees. We saw the signs of the logging that had taken place here during the early 20th century, including holes in trunks where planks were inserted for the loggers to stand on while they cut.

The trail finally left the woods in the last few hundred yards, as it rose up to the little knob, covered with lupine and other shrubs. Four benches were lined up, facing west to the ocean a couple miles away. Stopping for lunch, we looked down the Palo Colorado canyon, and the steep Long Valley Road to the north. There's a thickly forested valley to the south, and a bare ridgeline beyond that. To the west, the hills rolled away toward the ocean below us. Vultures made lazy circles just above our heads, and the sun on our faces felt good after the long walk in the shade.

I was surprised that the trail was obviously downhill heading back, as the slope was gradual. It really did not seem like climbing as we approached the bench and end point. Since

we were taking our time, stopping to watch the waterfalls and look for elusive creatures, the hike back took nearly an hour and a half, so a reasonable time for the whole hike, including lunch would be 3.5 hours, but could be done in much less time.

As in driving up the road, going back down is best done slowly and with headlights in operation. The road is narrow, has many turns and the view ahead is often blocked by large trees along the road.

I suggest an after hike refreshment stop at Rocky Point Restaurant, about a quarter mile north of Palo Colorado Road. Lunches are expensive, but a drink on the patio, overlooking storm ravaged rocks and tide pools, makes a fitting end to the trip.

Getting there: Drive approximately 10 miles south from Rio Road in Carmel on Highway 1 toward Big Sur. Look for Palo Colorado Canyon Road about ¼ mile past Rocky Point Restaurant. Turn left on Palo Colorado Canyon Road. The entrance to Mill Creek Preserve is located approximately 6.8 miles east of Highway 1. Drive very slowly and carefully. Parking is available on the shoulder of the road adjacent to the entrance to the trail.

14 Andrew Molera Park: Something for everyone (Jan/Feb 2012)

My first memory of Andrew Molera State Park was from the early 70s. The park was a recent addition to the State system and still unimproved. The parking lot and most of the trails were not in place. The old dirt road, through the meadow to the beach was a remnant from when the park was a working ranch.

We walked the mile to the beach and the mouth of the Big Sur River. Even then, the surfers had discovered it, and three guys with boards were camped out on the headland at the point. Otherwise, the area was deserted. The park was a chaos of meadow and forest. I imagined it to be as it was when the Esselen Indians had it to themselves.

In 1834 Juan Bautista Alvarado, the future governor of California, got a land grant of almost 9,000 acres from the Mexican government. This land changed hands and was eventually handed down to E.J. Molera, whose son was Andrew Molera.

It was a working farm, dairy and cattle ranch for many years. Upon Andrew's death, his sister Frances took control of the property, selling it to the Nature Conservancy in 1965, while retaining occupancy and grazing privileges until her death in 1968. The land was transferred to the State, but remained a working ranch until 1972, about the time I first visited.

The park has 24 walk in camp sites about a third of a mile from the parking lot. Having to walk to camp discourages people with heavy camping gear, so one can find a site at Molera when other areas are full. While camp sites are $10, day use is $6, and you can also park on the highway and walk in.

There are nearly 30 miles of trails in the park. Many people simply walk from the parking lot to the beach, a two mile round trip, on a choice of three trails. For the adventurous hiker who wants spectacular views, the Ridge/ Bluff 7 plus mile loop is outstanding. The preferred route, and the one we took, is to cross the river and take the River Trail to the Hidden Trail. In summer there's a bridge over the river by the parking lot, but during the winter, you take off your boots and wade through some very chilly water. Then, an almost flat walk along the River trail leads to the Hidden Trail, where you start a steep three quarters of a mile climb to the Ridge Trail. Then it's a gradual climb, another .8 mile on a dirt road to the top, at over 1,000 foot elevation. Along the way there is a stand of redwoods, about three quarters of the way up, a cool place to stop and admire the irises and other wild flowers.

There's a bench at the top, affording a view of the park, Point Sur, Pico Blanco and Post Summit. It's a great place for photography and lunch. Late winter and early spring is the best time to hike here. The air is clear and the visibility seems almost unlimited. From the bench, Point Sur and the lighthouse seems almost directly below, along with Molera Point and the mouth of the river.

Unfortunately, on the last hike here, we encountered a "meet up" group of about 30, who took over the bench and surrounding hillside, leaving us to hop the fence to the private land of Clear Ridge. we ate our lunch there, overlooking Pfeiffer Beach.

When hiking up the long, almost straight Ridge Trail, the return is via the Bluff Trail, which wanders down toward the beach, just left of the bench. The trail winds through wild flowers and coastal brush, none of it high enough to block the ocean views. It affords a continually stunning panorama, and there is a side trail, Spring Trail, to a secluded pocket beach. The bluff trail wanders steeply down, occasionally climbing again and then wandering over a dune area before descending to the beach.

Just before hitting the beach, after the trail becomes an old dirt road, there's a cut off to the Creamery Meadow trail, a short mile back to the river crossing. There's no sign at the junction, but it is obvious. For those wanting a bit more, the Bluff Trail continues down to the beach at the mouth of the Big Sur. From there, the beach trail parallels the Creamery Trail, but closer to the river. Another alternative is to cross the river near the mouth, which also is bridged only in summer, and head back the mile, along the river and through the campground to the parking lot. However, whenever I take that route, I have to make a short side trip up to the headland that hooks around the river mouth, a place of great views of the rolling Big Sur hills. The Beach, itself, is a great place to stop and relax and watch the waves wrap around the point and meet the outgoing river.

Going back the Creamery Meadow Trail, you pass the bottom of the Ridge Trail, another option for getting to the top. This trail is multi use: hikers, bikes and horses. The Ridge Trail, like The Creamery Meadow, is left over from the ranching days forty years ago.

There is also a trail on the east side of the highway, a few dozen yards south of the entrance. This climbs almost 1600

brutal feet in 2.5 miles before exiting the park. It continues on another 2 miles and 1600 more feet to the top of Post Summit. This is a very strenuous hike, best saved for a cool day. The sweeping views from Post Summit, along with looking down at circling hawks, almost make you forget the pain of the climb.

For people who want to explore without hiking, Molera Horseback Tours will guide you along the river, meadows and along the beach. You can reserve a horse in advance or simply show up.

Andrew Molera State Park has something for everyone, and it's only 20 miles from the Monterey Peninsula.

Getting there: Take Highway One to Carmel. After you pass the last Carmel signal at Rio Road, Molera is 20 miles down the scenic Big Sur Coast. The entrance sign is directly across the highway from the southern end of the Old Coast Road. There is ample parking along the road and in the parking lot.

15. Hiking with the (Medicine) Buddha (May/June 2012)

The Land of Medicine Buddha is buried in a redwood forested canyon in a corner of Soquel, near Santa Cruz. This spiritual retreat offers classes, free meditations, places to say, lovely temples, a swimming pool, a campground and a delightfully meditative hike. There are actually two hikes, a short, 1.2 mile, Eight Verses loop, with eight stations where one can stop, sit on a bench and ponder words of wisdom. The longer trail, the real hike, takes off from the mid-point of the short trail for a total of almost 6 miles.

The Eight Verses is a short loop within the longer loop, and you come upon it at the start or end of the hike, depending upon where you start. My preferred route is to enjoy the buildings of Medicine Buddha and the Eight Verses first.

The Land of Medicine Buddha is at the end of the one lane Prescott Road. Cross the bridge, turn left and right again at the entrance sign. There is room for a dozen or more cars. One end of the trail is across from the right turn to the parking area. Adjoining the parking area is the meditation center and the store. You can buy books and prayer flags and some really great chocolate. A sign says to keep your voice down due to people meditation. Walk up the steep drive past the pool and some lovely temples to the trailheads, one past the last temple at the end of the paved road, and the other a bit below it, both clearly marked. These are the start of the Eight Verses trail.

This trail climbs and drops gently though a shaded redwood forest, with the eight stations, each with a bench, a verse and an explication of the verse by the Dalai Lama. Take a bit of time to read these words of wisdom and put yourself in the right frame of mind for the rest of the hike. At about the midpoint of this loop, a sign reads "Enchanted Forest." That is the trail you want.

A few yards into the Enchanted Forest, there is an odd shrine, built into a log, on a flat open area in the trees. This is a place where people have placed photos and other personal items. There are prayer flags hanging from a tree in front of the shrine. It is an interesting place to stop and look at all the things placed over the years. Once past that, the wide trail climbs into the dense forest. You have hiked in the shade since the start, and it is doubtful you will need sunglasses again until you get back to the parking area.

After a few minutes, the trail starts to level off in a mixed forest, and soon you come to a place where the trail makes a right turn at a grove with prayer flags strung between trees. There is a tiny Buddha shrine on a tree, beyond the prayer flags, and you can walk past the flags and take a steep short cut trail back down to the loop trail. But you want to continue past the flags and along the ridge. You have now committed yourself to the six mile loop which continues to meander along the ridge under the dappled light of a dense mixed forest.

The trail continues to climb gently along a ridge. To the right is The Forest of Nisene Marks, and to the left, you can occasionally look into the populated valley in which the San Jose/Soquel Road leads to Summit Road, which is the border between Santa Cruz and Santa Clara Counties.

As you continue along the ridge, you come to a split in the trail. Keep to the left: You will see a red arrow painted on a tree. The trail, now only a single track, climbs again, steeply in a few places until it climbs high on the ridge to approximately 1,000 feet in elevation, and turns sharply west again. From there you start to descend, and after a short downhill, you reach another junction. The right will take you to Nisene Marks and out to the trail-head at the end of Olive Springs Road, but go straight, on the left fork, to get back down to Medicine Buddha. It was at this junction, unsure about where we were, that we ran into people coming up from Medicine Buddha and also someone coming from Olive Springs. We all gave each other directions, so no one got lost. If you want a longer hike, walk out to the right and explore that corner of the state park.

Here is where the trail gets interesting, with a series of turns and switch backs, as it steadily drops out of the mixed forest and deeper into the redwoods. In time you step over the headwaters of Bates Creek, before continuing down to the forest floor. Keep your eyes open for the occasional banana slug along the trail.

Patterns of light filter through the trees as you walk above the creek, and soon you spot the Eight Verses trail on the other side of the creek, which flows below you. At one point the trail is muddy and very narrow, requiring careful footing as you climb and drop again. Another trail goes uphill to the left. Ignore it and keep going right, and soon you come out on the road, just below the parking area. A sharp left takes you back to the car. Remember, if you start from this end, at every place I previously mentioned, to take the left fork, you would now take the right.

If you do the six mile loop, you only see half the Eight Verses trail. So, if you still have energy, go back to the trailhead and explore the other half of that loop, being sure to absorb the timeless wisdom of the other verses.

For those not in a hurry, it is soothing to just sit down on one of those benches, in front of a verse, pull out your snack and take in the total peace and quiet of the place. Even though this trail is fairly popular on weekends, it is almost always dead silent.

Whichever direction you choose to hike, take a few minutes to wander the grounds of The Land of Medicine Buddha, check out the temples, sound the bell and turn the prayer wheels (they encourage you to do that). I find that this sets the mellow mood for the hike.

Getting there: Exit Highway One at the Porter/Bay exit (Capitola/Soquel exit), south of Santa Cruz, and go east a very short block to main Street. Turn right and continue past the signal at Soquel Drive. Drive up Main to the junction of Glen Haven, where you take the right fork. At Prescott, take the right fork again for a mile of one lane road, remembering to turn on your headlights. The Land of Medicine Buddha is at the end of the road.

16 Castle Rock: Nature preserved (July/Aug 2012)

Douglas fir, madrone, seven kinds of oak and groves of redwoods, combined with sweeping views all the way to Point Sur, make Castle Rock State Park not only a natural wonder, but a place begging to be saved from state park closure.

Fortunately, this park will be saved due to $250,000 donation, enough to keep it open for another year. This from the Sempervirens Fund, a non-profit conservation group in Los Altos. This donation is expected to pay the salary and health benefits of one full-time ranger, one full-time maintenance person and several part-time summer seasonal park aides.

An extra benefit, this arrangement will also open 1,340 acres on the park's southern boundary that have been closed to the public for more than a decade. This allows access to more miles of hiking trails.

There will also be a new park entrance on Summit Road, allowing more parking.

Cheering the good news and realizing it has been awhile since I explored the park, I gathered a couple of friends to go hiking one early spring day, a longer trip from the coast than from the Santa Clara Valley. The park actually sits on the ridgeline of the Santa Cruz mountains on the Santa Clara-Santa Cruz county line, near the intersection of Highway 9 and 35 (Skyline

Drive).

From the parking lot, walking past the restrooms, we started down the Saratoga Gap Trail, (at about elevation 3,000 ft.), toward Castle Rock Falls and just under a mile down the wooded hill, along a creek. A short way down, an unmarked trail went up to the left, leading to the park's namesake rock. Continuing down the wide trail, we crossed a wooden bridge and found a junction. The Ridge Trail went up on the right toward Goat Rock. We took that and climbed up the trail, along the side of a ridge, which offered some impressive views.

There were places along the trail that required careful stepping up and over rock formations and boulders, and at one point the trail seemed to go straight, but suddenly ended at a rock pile followed by a steep drop. The actual trail goes uphill on the right, a bit obscure at first, but soon an obvious trail.

About a half mile from the junction, you arrive at Goat Rock, one of the popular climbing rocks in the park. This chunk of sandstone looks like a giant piece of Swiss cheese, and a series of steps lead climbers to the base. Another set of steps on the right leads up behind the top of the rock and the continuation of the Ridge Trail.

Above the rock, the trails diverge. The one on the right is a short spur to the Interpretive Center, a visit to which only adds two tenths of a mile to your hike. The left trail is the Ridge Trail to the campground.

Another trail leads a short way off to the left to a scenic overlook, well worth a stop. The Santa Cruz Mountains are spread out below, along with stretches of the ocean and a view, on a clear day, of Point Sur, 60 miles away.

There are other spurs leading to scenic overlooks, all worth the few steps, particularly if you have a camera. Looking out over the forest below, you might see circling hawks, vultures an possibly an eagle.

The Ridge Trail heads through oak-studded meadows, past the other trail to the Interpretive Center, before heading down again through manzanitas, ceanothus, coffeeberry, chamise, pitcher sage, toyon and more large stands of madrone.

After dropping down this trail for a half mile or more, you will come to a junction. The right will take you to the campground and beyond to Saratoga Gap, Big Basin State Park and eventually to the beach, some 30 miles away. To add some distance to the hike, without a back pack trip, you can go the other mile and a half to the campground before returning. Otherwise, turn left back toward the parking lot, via the falls.

This return trip offers more sweeping views along with views of the interesting sandstone rocks above. There are a few places where the trail climbs over some rocks, so care must be taken to avoid a painful fall.

After a half mile, the trail moves into the forest again, and you come upon the Castle Rock Falls Overlook, a deck built out over the rocks. The little falls drops just below you. Just past the deck, there are some impromptu trails people have made to the top of the falls. Park signs warn against the temptation to go there.

About a quarter mile further completes the loop at the Ridge Trail junction and the climb back through the woods to the parking lot.

When you get to that unmarked trail, now on your right, make a side trip, adding about a half mile, to check out Castle Rock. It stands in the open and is usually assaulted by groups of climbers. This trail will take you to the rock, and will continue on to the parking lot, so you do not have to retrace your steps. Another similar rock is just off the main trail and just below the parking lot, another clump of Swiss cheese sandstone.

If you find this park worthy of saving, remember that Sempervirens Fund, which started the state park system in 1902 by saving the redwood land that became Big Basin, is looking for more private donations to fund its Castle Rock efforts.

Depending on your side trips, the hike will be between three and a half and six and a half miles.

Also there are additional trails heading toward the Partridge Farm and on to the noisy Gun Club. Across the road is Sanborn County Park and the Skyline Trail-Bay Area Ridge Trail. You can easily spend a full day here.

Getting there: There are several ways to get to Castle Rock. From Los Gatos/Saratoga, take Highway 9, which has an exit off Highway 17, and continue on 9, which becomes Big Basin Way as it goes up the hill. Turn left at the top of the ridge, Skyline Blvd. to the parking lot.

You can also exit Highway 17 at Summit Road, a narrow, twisting road that leads to Skyline Dr. From Santa Cruz, the easiest route is up Highway 9, through the San Lorenzo Valley to Skyline.

17. Coastal Hike with Scenic Falls (Marin, Sept/Oct 2012)

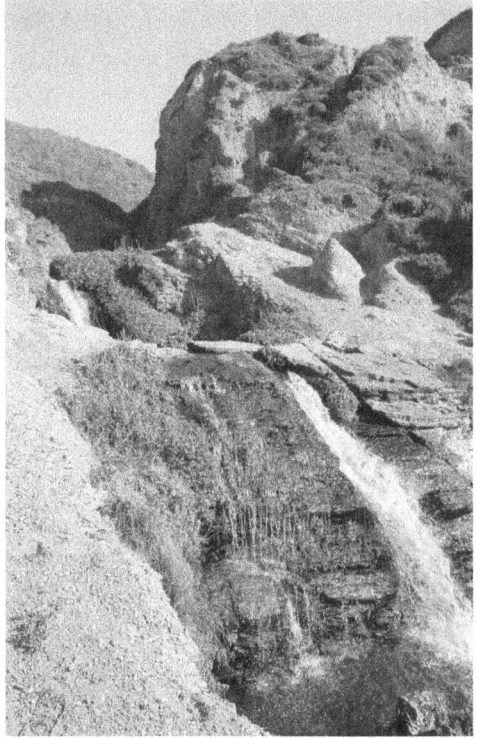

Waterfalls that fall directly on a beach are as rare as they are fascinating. While the most popular and most accessible is the much photographed McWay Falls in Big Sur, there is another comparable falls, requiring a good hike. Alamere Falls is located in the Point Reyes National Seashore in West Marin. It is actually four falls, three small ones above the beach, and the main falls, a long drop to the sand.

The trail is well off the beaten track, but popular just the same. You have to get to Bolinas off Highway One, near Stinson Beach, then drive over four miles out Mesa Road to the Palomarin trailhead. In my opinion, the trip is worth it, as the falls and the vistas along the way are both scenic and stunning.

I was surprised to find a small crowd on that cold December weekday, with almost a dozen cars in the lot. While there were a number of day hikers, there were two parties loading for a backpacking trip. The several camps in the area require a back country permit for camping.

Getting ahead of a group of packers, I climbed the 17 steps from the lot to the trailhead and was on my way on a trail wide enough for a jeep. Almost immediately I found myself in a grove of huge eucalyptus trees, and within five minutes I had exited the grove. The trail arched inland around a shallow canyon with a tiny creek. There was also a short cutoff down into the canyon, over the creek and up the other side.

From there, the trail ran along the bluff for at least a mile, offering sweeping views of some of the most majestic stretches of the north coast. Duxbury Reef to the south and Point Reyes to the north. The trail gradually climbed and then dropped again as it went inland around a wider and deeper canyon. It crossed a creek on a bridge before starting back up the other side. There was a long uphill, almost another mile, which accounted for the reported 400 foot elevation gain. After climbing up the north side of the canyon, the trail left the coast and entered a forest of pine, fir and bay, with ferns carpeting the forest floor. At one point I passed a line of what appeared to be Douglas Fir, like the remains of an old Christmas tree farm.

I came to a trail junction at 2.2 miles from the trailhead. The ridge Trail was to the right, and the falls were to the left, toward the ocean. In another 3 or 4 minutes I was above a small pond, choked with plants. A few minutes later I passed above Bass Lake, a clear, inviting lake. I could hear the stream rushing down to steep slope to the lake as I passed an old trough with a sign saying, "Not potable water."

I was now heading downhill. At the northern end of the lake there was a trail heading down to the lake. Had it been a warm September day, rather than winter, I might have wandered down to take a swim, as many do.

Shortly after passing Bass Lake, while continuing downhill, I passed above another good-sized lake, calm and blue, Pelican Lake. It was somewhere near Pelican Lake that I passed another sign, at a trail that was now closed. It informed me that I was 3.1 miles from the trailhead, with perhaps a mile left to go.

Continuing downhill and out into the open, with views of Point Reyes, I came to the junction for which I had been waiting. Unlike the wide trail on which I had been, this was a narrow, single track sandwiched between rows of brush. It said .4 miles to the falls, that it was an unmaintained trail, and dangerous.

The trail dropped fairly steeply toward the bluffs, alternating between walls of foliage and open vistas. When I reached a place above the falls, I saw what unmaintained actually meant. A badly rutted steep section, requiring careful footing and hand bracing, led down to the upper falls. These were three short falls, none higher than 8 or 9 feet. The trail crossed above the bottom of these, requiring a short hop over the creek.

I was now on a flat bluff. The creek ran from the falls I had just crossed to the edge of the bluff and over to the beach, perhaps 40 or 50 feet below. I walked to the edge; it was a straight drop. I knew people had viewed the falls from the beach, so I walked around a bit. I spotted the trail about 100 feet north.

This is where it became problematic. I climbed about half way down the trail, and at a point perhaps 25 feet above the beach, there was a ledge with a drop of close to five feet. I sat on the ledge and analyzed the situation. The rest of the trail was on loose talus, and there were no noticeable hand holds. At the bottom of the initial drop, the trail dropped down to the beach at about a 45 degree angle, loose and slippery looking.

Two thoughts ran through my head. First, if I were to drop and my foot slipped on landing, I would tumble all the way to the beach, possibly breaking a leg. If that did not happen and I bottom slid down to the sand, would be able to scramble up the ledge?

Had I come with someone else, I would not have hesitated. Two people helping each other could handle it safely, albeit carefully. To my knowledge, I was alone. I saw myself, with a freezing night

approaching, stranded on the beach, possibly injured, so I missed the chance to get a full frontal shot of the falls. I settled, instead, to leaning out over the bluff to get a side shot. My suggestion, unless you are a confident climber, make this trip with at least one other person.

Leaving the falls, I ran into a young woman who said she saw what appeared to be a wolf. I suggested that perhaps it was a coyote, and that seemed to make sense to her. For my part, the most exotic creature I saw was a very large garter snake crossing the trail.

As I got close to the trailhead, I ran into a small group headed for Wildcat Camp, a popular campground 5.5 miles further. I did not realized until talking to these men that while Wildcat was about a mile past the falls turn off, one could walk along the beach from the camp to the falls, avoiding the slippery drop.

The round trip is claimed to be as long as 8.8 miles and as short as 7.7 miles. My guess is that it was not over 8 total miles, since I had gotten a late start, and in my hurry did it in less than four hours. I would advise allowing four and a half to five hours, including a stop at the falls for lunch, longer if you take in Wildcat Camp.

Getting There: Palomarin Trailhead is near Bolinas, off Hwy 1. The Bolinas turn off at Olema-Bolinas Road, is unmarked, about the 17.5 mile post after leaving the 101, just north of the Golden Gate Bridge. Turn left on the first road north of the lagoon. Go a mile to the stop sign (the farm stand), turn left past the school. At the next stop, Mesa, turn right and drive to the end of the road (4.5 miles). If you enter Bolinas, you've passed Mesa.

18. Pinnacles: Rocks and Wildflowers (Nov/Dec 2012)

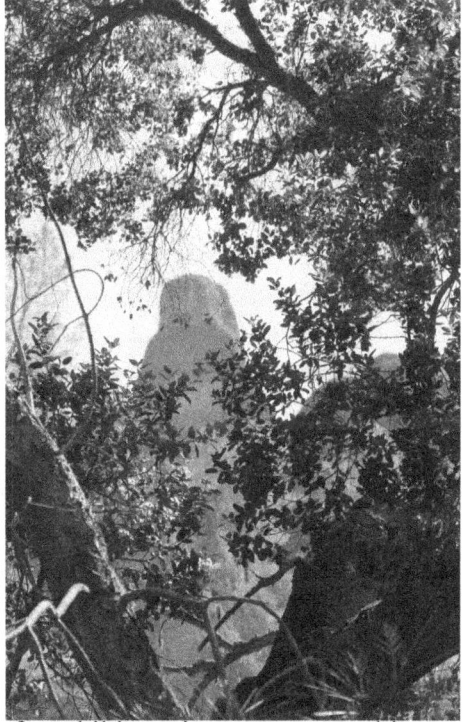

There are two good reasons for not hiking Pinnacles National Monument in summer: The stifling heat and the lack of wildflowers. However, spring is delightful in this geological anomaly, a piece of land dragged here from down south due to the unrelenting forces of plate tectonics. Pinnacles is part of a 25 million year old volcano, originating near Lancaster in the southern California desert.

By picking mid-May for a hiking trip, we were pushing the season, not sure if the flowers were still out and also not clear about the weather. We did find abundant flowers, but the heat, around 90 degrees, left us wilted after a few hours.

Trying to get a fairly early start from the Santa Cruz area, the over an hour and a half drive brought us to the park at 10AM, just as the heat arrived. From the parking lot, we took the right hand trail toward the High Peaks Trail, which at first followed a small stream and was shaded in sections.

This pleasant uphill provided spectacular views of the high peak rock formations, set against wisps of residual clouds left over from the morning fog. It also took us along patches of wild sweet pea, sticky monkey flower, thistles and other flowers.

As we left the canyon and the stream and started up the bare, exposed rock of the High Peaks Trail, the sun climbed high into the sky, and the temperature climbed with it. Being uncomfortable and knowing we wanted some energy and time left for the Balconies Cave Trail, we turned back before wandering through the maze of rock formations near the top.

Back at the parking lot, we refilled our almost empty water bottles and headed out the trail to the left, which also featured running water and patches of meadow strewn with flowers.

We found a rock with a level sitting area, perfect for a lunch stop and just a few feet off the trail. There, with a bit of shade from a small grove of trees we shared our lunch with a brazen stellers jay, obviously used to being fed by visitors.

The trail splits about a half mile from the parking lot, and we started climbing the balconies, which leveled off below a massive rock wall, perfect for experienced rock climbers, but definitely not suitable for hikers. In fact, all along the trails in the park there are signs indicating where people can rock climb. Along the trail we found the last blooms of Indian Paint Brush clinging to the sides of the trail. At the top of the balconies, there were paths out on the overhanging rocks, offering a look back west into the canyon, between steep walls of rock.

After about a mile along the rock face, the trail brought us back down to a junction. The West Fork Chalone Creek Trail heads east over three miles to the East Pinnacles Ranger Station and parking. Turning right, leads to the Balconies Caves, giving us our one chance to cool.

There is a gate that can be locked on the way to the caves, should floods or unstable rocks make them unsafe. The short walk to the caves took us along Chalone Creek and sometimes

through it. At the entrance to the caves, we tightened up our camera and other packs and put on our head lamps; some sort of flashlight is mandatory for negotiating the caves. There are only two, fairly short, sections that are very dark and narrow, but without light, you can not get through. Between these sections, there is a fairly open section that quickly narrows down before plunging into the darkness again.

After exiting the caves, a short but tiring trek, given the places where we had to climb up rocks in tight places, we were out in the narrow canyon, again by the creek, for a short walk back to the junction.

From there, it's about a half mile to the parking lot, but it was now 2PM, and the hottest part of the day. We were passing fewer hikers now, even though it was a Saturday and still officially spring. We got back, splashed water on our faces, took off our packs and climbed into an air conditioned car for the ride back down narrow and winding route 146.

On the way out, we made a quick stop at the brand new visitors center, at the park entrance. It replaced the one at the trail head parking lot, and it looks like a spot suitable for a new campground, something that's gone missing from the park for many years. The only camping is in a private camp ground on the east side.

For the five to five and a half miles we hiked, late spring is doable. However, there are longer and hotter trails that are perfect for earlier in the spring or even fall or winter. Among those, the North wilderness trail which heads out to the left of the parking lot and picnic area, makes a 7 mile loop up into the higher country, along the north fork of Chalone Creek. It meets with the west fork about a mile east of the caves.

There are a couple loops in the High Peaks, with one leading to East Pinnacles. As you climb to the top, look down, and the parking lot is directly below you. You can also take the fork toward the Bear Gulch Day Use Area on the east side, with a side loop to the Bear Gulch Cave Trail. And, if you feel ambitious, another 3.3 miles will take you to 3304 Ft. North Chalone Peak. But again, you'll want to do that before May, when the weather is a bit more forgiving.

If you venture to the High Peaks or Chalone Peak, particularly in early morning or late afternoon, you might catch sight of a rare condor, a member of the vulture family, with a wing span of ten feet. Brought back from near extinction by a captive breeding program, they are now thriving in small numbers at the Pinnacles and near Big Sur.

For those coming from a distance, the Pinnacles Campground is located east of and just outside the park. For reservations, please visit recreation.gov or call (877) 444-6777. The campground also has a camp store.

Getting there from the west is easy. Take Hwy 101 through the Salinas Valley to Hwy 146 at Soledad, about 25 miles south of Salinas. Follow the signs for 146 and Pinnacles for about 10 miles to the park. From the east, take Hwy 25 south out of Hollister to the East Pinnacles cut off, also Hwy 146. Unfortunately, this highway doesn't go through the park.

19. Breathtaking Point Arena: New public lands (Jan/Feb 2013)

When people talk about a perfect day, I usually take it with a grain of salt. However, Nov. 3, 2012 came about as close to being as perfect as it gets for an outdoor lover. First, picture Point Arena, California in November. You'll likely think about cold fog, wind, rain or some combination. Everyone who attended the event that day was surprised at the clear, windless day with temperatures in the seventies.

This event, billed as a hike, whale-watch and volunteer outing with the California Wilderness Coalition, brought people from all over central and northern California. It brought me up from Santa Cruz County. The purpose of the gathering was to show people a great slice of coastal land, with a missing piece that may be purchased very soon and added to public land. There is also the hope that we can make this stretch of coastal bluff the first onshore piece of the California Coastal National Monument, and trust me, it deserves that designation.

Ryan Henson, a long time organizer for Cal Wild, was the point person on this. There were also people, such as Jeff

Fontana, from the Bureau of Land Management, as well as Lindsey Kraatz and Christine Anterson from Representative Mike Thompson's office.

Thompson has introduced a bill, H.R. 4969 on April 27, 2012 with Congresswoman Lynn Woolsey. This bill would expand the California Coastal National Monument to include public lands owned by the Bureau of Land Management in the Point Arena-Stornetta area. This bill is awaiting a vote in the House Committee on Natural Resources. Senators Boxer and Feinstein introduced a companion bill in the Senate in September. Another option would be for President Obama, using his authority under the Antiquities Act, to designate it as part of the monument.

After a night camped out, with only the sound of the ocean, I met up with the group of over twenty people at the Point Arena City Hall. Over coffee and cookies, several people spoke about the property we were going to explore, the reasons to put it in public ownership and some information about the national monument.

We grabbed our lunches and exited the parking lot and on to the coastal bluffs, stopping to eat high above the Point Arena cove, looking down at fishing boats bobbing on a calm, blue

cove. We then started our walk, about four miles to Lighthouse Road, near the scenic Point Arena Light Station.

As we walked along the edge of the bluff, we watched waves break over the rock reefs and through the many sea arches. This coast has been sculpted by the waves for a millennia and is constantly changing, as we soon saw for ourselves.

After walking out to the first point, someone spotted humpback whales outside the

kelp line, and
with binocu-
lars raised,
we watched
these graceful
giants undu-
late through
the swells.
And when we
turned our

eyes back to the land, a Great Blue Heron was standing on the
edge of the bluff.

We continued wandering the web of bluff trails until we
came to an opening in a fence. There was a sign indicating that
the right to pass was subject to the control of the owner, Cypress
Abbey Company. Permission had been specifically obtained for
this day's hike. The owners can be touchy, so until the sale is fi-
nalized, hike this section at your own risk. This was the piece of
land to hopefully be purchased as the final section of the over ten
miles stretch of open space that would extend past the lighthouse,
the Garcia River, Manchester State Park and all the way to Alder
Creek. The seller is willing, and the Trust for Public Lands is
putting together the funding, with lobbying help from Conserva-
tion Lands Foundation and California Wilderness Coalition.

Passing another open gate further up, we saw some old
buildings, formerly a LORAN Station, now connected to the
local community college. LORAN is a land-based navigational
system once operated by the Coast Guard; it has been replaced
by GPS.

At one bend in the bluff, nearing Sea Lion Rocks, one of
the locals diverted the group to a couple of places near the point.
There we found two blow holes. Waves had carved caves way
below us, and when a wave surged in, air would be pushed out
through the holes with enough force to blow hair straight up from
the head. We were reminded of the effects of constant erosion in
the area. In fact, a bit further we walked by a large sink hole with
a small tunnel to the ocean. One day in the not too distant future,

this will be a narrow land bridge which will eventually collapse, making this sink hole into another of the many pocket bays along the coast.

At one point we crossed a small creek and followed it to the edge of the bluff. It ended in a small waterfall to nowhere, disappearing into cracks in the coastal rock.

About four miles into our coastal walk, we went through a BLM stile at Lighthouse Road, where some of our party had erected the frame for a public land sign. Some of us hopped into a BLM pickup and drove out to the end of the road, dug a hole and erected a small "Conserving California's Coastal Treasures" sign, explaining the Marine Protected Areas. This was adjacent to the lighthouse museum, where you can take a tour for $7.50.

I found that doing a small amount of work on the sign highly rewarding, a way of giving back in exchange for the wonderful experience I'd had that day and for a future where this entire scenic stretch is open for the public's enjoyment.

The final piece of open space will be about three times longer, more miles of sea arches, caves and coves, streams and rock reefs, birds, butterflys and flowers. In fact the Behren Silverspot Butterfly and the Point Arena Mountain Beaver are two endangered creatures who only live along this piece of coast.

Come out and explore, starting along Lighthouse Road or at Point Arena's city hall. Follow it up with a hike at Manchester State Beach or just south of Point Arena at Bowling Ball Beach.

Plan to stay over, as this area, between the Russian and Navarro Rivers, called the Mendonoma Coast requires a long winding drive from the 101 corridor.

20. Super Hike Sunday: Point Buchon Trail (May/June 2013)

As soon as I heard about this trail, I knew I had to go, this area being a slice of my personal coastal terra incognita, one of my exploration fantasies. The first convenient day to make the three hour drive to the trailhead was Super Bowl Sunday, and I figured that the game would make both the trail and the highway less crowded, and even though I passed many groups of people, I did manage to have a long stretch of trail all to myself.

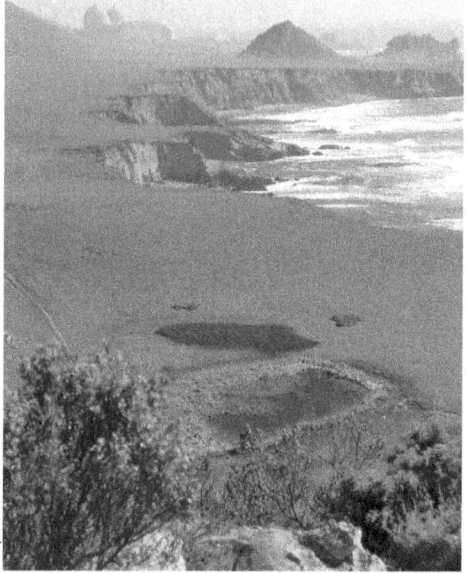

My first surprise, after driving to the end of the road in Montana de Oro State Park, was that this trail had been open for five years, a fact apparently well known by locals. I parked in the last lot in the state park and walked through the gate onto Pacific Gas and Electric (PG &E) property, down the hill, over the Coon Creek Bridge and back up to the check-in station. Every visitor must sign a waiver before hiking, promising to stay on the designated trail and be back by 3:45 PM.

After driving almost 150 miles in fog and mist, I was pleasantly surprised to see the Montana de Oro area clear and sunny, with enough wind to blow the few clouds well inland.

The first part of the trail is a loop, the right fork leading to Coon Creek Beach, the only beach access on the trail. The creek runs down the middle of the sandy beach, and the rocky headland at the northern end of the beach has a huge cave to explore, if the tide is low enough.

Above the beach, where the trail turns south, there is a sinkhole with a fence around it, along with warning signs. Looking down, I saw the opening to the sea, the waves surging in and out. From here on the trail follows the coastline, and in a short way a side trail leads quiickly up to the Point Buchon lookout area, complete with a bench and a resident hawk in the tower. Here I could look south along the storm-tossed, rocky shore, the large winter waves crashing against the jagged sea stacks and through the many arches and natural bridges.

Just past the point a trail back to the check-in station, across the meadow, was clearly marked. That would be my return route. Following the coastal bluffs south, my next stop was Disney/Fat Point, with a short side trail to a lookout spot. A sign said that I'd gone 1.5 miles, with 1.9 more to go. Looking along the coast, I realized that this piece of coast rivaled, in its dramatic beauty, the wonderful coastal bluffs of Point Arena

The trail, which is an old dirt road along the bluffs, continued to another small, unnamed point, before angling away from the coastal bluffs. The next map destination was Big Wash, a gully coming down from a wildly eroded section of the hills.

At about this point, the trail turned away from the road and became a single track path, moving up a hillside meadow with sweeping coastal views and grazing cattle. The trail gradually climbed, running along the side of a steep hill, just below an electrified fence before coming to Windy Point.

I got the impression that Windy Point was the final destination for many hikers, as this was the anticipated view and beyond the point, the trail seemed less traveled. Windy Point has a bench and the only other restrooms beside the ones at the trailhead. Once I arrived, I knew why this point got its name. Also, from this point on, I was the only hiker on the trail.

The best part of Windy Point is the view south. A long, steep, brilliantly green meadow stretched ahead for over a half mile, and directly below me was Tom's Pond, probably a watering hole for the cattle. But, further ahead, beyond the next ridge,

a soft, flat gray in the distance, was the Diablo Canyon Nuclear Power Plant, looking like some abstract Turkish temple, with its two onion-shaped towers. This, I discovered, was the place to see the plant, as once I dropped below Windy Point, I lost sight of it.

The trail hung alongside of the steep meadow, just below the fence and the ranch road, staying high until dropping to the next low ridge. From there the trail dropped sharply before crossing a road. Then a sign said that I was approaching the end of the trail, and I could see posts, signs and a bench just ahead.

By now I had passed through three or four stiles in the series of electrified fencing, the final one was just as I passed the last road. And now at the end of the trail, there was not only a sign saying this was the point to turn around, but also a sign saying that the power plant was ahead and the security people would use deadly force to protect it. I got the message: this was as far as I go, some 3.4 miles from the check-in point.

After chasing my hat in the wind and stopping at the bench to have a bite of lunch, it was time to head back. Even though I was retracing the same route, the views in the other direction were every bit as impressive as those coming in.

After passing Windy Point, the afternoon wind even stronger, I had to share the trail with some cows, which fortunately were easy to shoo out of my way.

On the return route, I was paying more attention to the birds, including hawks, egrets, sparrows, gulls and vultures. I was also enjoying the early blooming of the California Poppies along the trails.

Even though the trail rose and dropped, there were no sections that were particularly steep, the steepest part was the short hike up from the Coon Creek Bridge to the Check-in station. The official distance from check-in to the end is 3.4 miles, but when you add in a detour to the beach and the short walk from the parking lot, you've done at least seven miles. If in a hurry, the hike can be done in three hours, but that doesn't count exploring the beach and stopping for lunch. Best to allow three and a half to four hours.

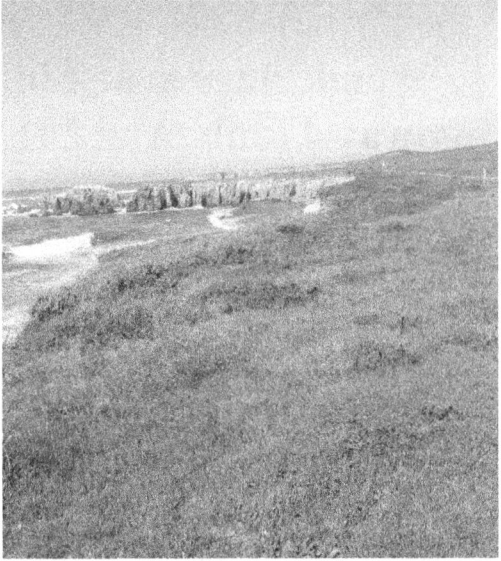

Getting there:To get to Point Buchon, take the Los Osos exit (Los Osos Valley Rd.) off Highway 101, just south of San Luis Obispo and continue through Los Osos to Montana de Oro State Park. Drive through the park to the last parking lot. Coming from the north, you can take the Los Osos/Baywood Park exit off Highway 1 (So. Bay Blvd), just south of Morro Bay to Los Osos Valley Rd, and turn right to the park. The trail is closed Tuesday and Wednesday, and visitors are limited to 275 per day, so come early.

21. Wanderings near Ebbetts Pass by Highway 4 (July/Aug 2013)

The Pacific Crest Trail goes, well, it just about goes on forever. Just past the trail head at Ebbetts Pass, we ran into a fellow who had been on the trail for a month, starting near Dunsmuir and headed toward Mt. Whitney. We weren't that ambitious, camping down the road at Pacific Valley and day hiking a few selected trails.

We did head north on the trail, climbing steeply upward below Ebbetts Peak at first. Upward always seems to be the case in the Sierra, particularly when you've just arrived at 8,700 feet after living at sea level.

Eastern Sierra vistas greeted us from rocky outcroppings on the way up, and then, as we entered the Mokelumne wilderness, we dropped again, and the trail skirted two small lakes, one being Sherrold Lake, with a small beach area that hinted that it might be a nice place to take a swim.

After a couple miles we could look down on upper and lower Kinney Lakes. There was a short trail leading down to upper, nestled in a bowl with granite outcroppings on the southern side.

Then the trail entered a wooded area again and ran along

some impressive granite cliffs before turning east and heading down to a long, lush meadow. To the left a steep, rugged ridge rose up, looking like it had an ancient volcanic origin. A wooded hillside dropped off to the right, with upper Kinney Lake far below.

After stopping to admire the meadow and have a bit of lunch, we walked on until the vista opened up at about two and a half to three miles in, the trail undulating along a vast open area. At that point we turned back.

That was a warm up hike to acclimate us to the altitude. However, since water is no longer available at Pacific Valley, we had to detour up to Alpine Lake to fill our jugs before returning to camp. There was a pump, but the handle was removed and the pump chained. The creek, which flowed around the edge of our campsite, was barely moving, so perhaps lack of water was the problem.

There was, however, enough water to keep the meadow next to our campsite lush and green, which provided forage for the small group of friendly horses that grazed there. They were probably connected to the cabin just west of the campground. These well-cared-for horses seemed anxious for us to stroke them, probably also expecting us to give them treats.

Above the end of the Pacific Valley campground, the old jeep road continues past a locked gate up to the head of the valley, through a rocky forest, where it connects to other trails to the high country. I explored a bit of this road before sunset one night.

The following day we drove a few miles west to Mosquito Lake, near Alpine Lake. From there a trail headed south and made a loop, coming out about four and a half mile later, further to the west. Again, we started with a long, steep uphill, a short downhill into the Carson/Iceberg Wilderness followed by another up, and so on. We finally dropped steeply down almost to a stream.

At that point there was a trail junction. Three miles would complete the loop, with a continuing down hill for a couple of miles followed by a one mile climb. The other fork lead a half mile up over a ridge and down to Heiser Lake, surrounded by

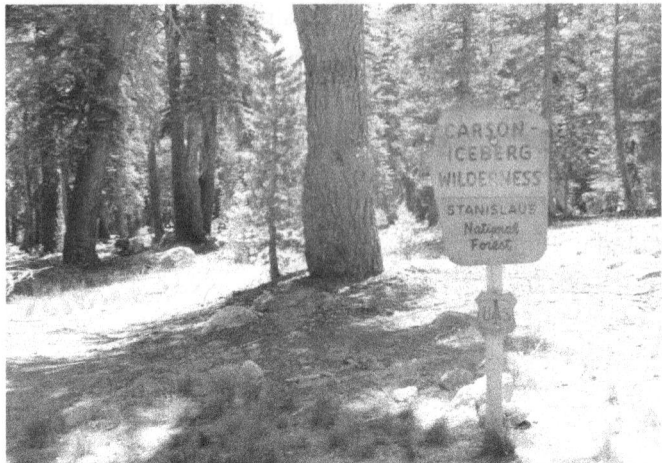

forests, granite boulders and green meadows. This small lake sits at 8353 ft, at a latitude of

38.4945991and longitude: -119.9063962. Shade, scenery and a soft breeze made this the perfect place to have lunch and day-dream.

When we got back to the junction, we voted to go back the way we came, so we headed up the very steep trail out of the valley and over the ridge, stopping to take in the sweeping views before dropping into the wooded valley and up over the final ridge.

After arriving at the car by Mosquito Lake, we were told about some deposits of mica in a shallow part of the lake. Looking down at these caught the light and sent beams of color up through the water, like tiny underwater lasers.

On day three, we drove to the trail head at Wolf Creek, forty minutes east on Hwy. 4, followed by fifteen minutes down the mostly unpaved Wolf Creek Road. The trail head is just above a campground, so there's a final toilet before getting on the trail. Wolf Creek is located at the East fork of the Carson River, and is located within the Carson/Iceberg Wilderness.

Rather than steep ups and downs, the Wolf Creek trail was mostly a steady uphill, following the creek. At first the valley was wide and forested, and then the canyon narrowed, with granite walls rising steeply on both sides. The river, not large, but rushing in places was always just below us on the left. The trail was wide and easy to follow, and at one point it came down almost to the river along a section of slick rock.

A bit further on the trail crossed two side streams fairly close together, one large enough to have small waterfalls, just the right height for filling canteens.

The trail then rose again, leaving the river perhaps a hundred feet below, and when it dropped again, there was a place to bushwhack down to the river. This was just below the confluence of two streams or two forks of the Wolf. Just over the creek, which could be crossed with great care or with good river sandals, there was a large, green meadow with almost filled in ancient ponds. Along this piece of river we found a campsite and fire ring, so we knew this was a good place to stop.

Off came the boots, and we had lunch as we soaked our feet in the cold stream. We figured that we'd come up the creek for about two and a half to three miles.

It was getting late, so we headed back, a pleasant downhill, although the temperature was at least 90 by mid afternoon, since it is only about 6,500 feet above sea level.

Actually, all of the hikes were done in high temperatures, mid 80s along the crest, due to a heat wave that hit about the time we arrived.

After a long drive back it was time to fix our final dinner before campfire stories and a good night sleep before the long drive home the next morning.

Getting there: Travel east on Highway 4 from Highway 99 near Stockton, CA, through Murphy's and Angels Camp until you see signs for the campgrounds mentioned in the article.

22. Sample the PCT at Big Bear Lake (Sept/Oct 2013)

The Annual Day Zero Pacific Crest Trail Kick Off, a massive event near San Diego in late April, is a gathering of people determined to hike the PCT from the Mexican to the Canadian border. This year, an estimated 1100 people signed up for this hike, and probably not much more than 10% will finish, but my hat is off to anyone who puts a dent in this 2,300 plus mile hike. More specifically, my hat's off to those who make it to Big Bear, somewhere near 150 miles. However, some serious hikers, those who don't want to walk with 1100 strangers, leave a few days earlier.

It was some of those serious, early birds that I ran into on a stretch of the PCT near Big Bear Lake in early May, hardy people who have committed to five months of walking and a half dozen pair of boots. I can't claim to be one of those with a backpack and a focus on the Canadian border. I was, however, taking a scenic hike along a short stretch. Our hike leader, Dan McKernan of the Big Bear Vistior's bureau drove us a couple miles up Polique Rd, off of North Shore Drive to give several journalists a sample, a teaser of the wonderful hiking opportunities in the area.

On that day, we hiked not much more than four miles, but

what a scenic hike it was. Heading northwest on the trail, we soon found ourselves above the shimmering, blue lake, Mount San Gorgornio, at 11,500 feet, the highest peak in Southern California, rising up across the valley. The lake and snow-capped mountains were visible for most of the hike. Along the way we learned how to tell a Ponderosa Pine from a Jeffery Pine, by their cones: Prickly Ponderosa, gentle Jeffery. Rubbing our hands up the cone told us immediately which it was. We also smelled the bark, as Ponderosa has a faintly vanilla odor. We also learned that the north side of the lake, while forested, was drier, with sparser vegetation, than the south, it being in the rain shadow.

Even though it has been a dry spring, there were a few wildflowers out, mostly Blue Lupine, Wallflowers and Indian Paint Brush. At around 7,600 feet, spring comes late on this stretch of trail, so more flowers will bloom in June There were many birds calling from the pines, but none that would stand still long enough to be identified. Lizards scurried across the trail, and we even caught a Western Skink, a lizard with a blazing blue tail, and one who didn't like being caught, as it bit Dan on the finger.

This particular section of trail rises gently until it gradually ascends to a ridgeline, which affords a view down to the, flat, green Holcomb Valley, easily recognized as the opening scene of the old TV show Bonanza and the setting for the film "Paint Your Wagon," among others. This valley is also the home of many active gold mining claims, which I visited later that day. It was interesting to be able to look down at the two valleys, both impressive in their own way, at the same time. Also, from the trail head, it would be an easy two mile hike further on Polique Road to Holcomb Valley.

We encountered several PCT backpackers along the way, several of whom said they deliberately got a head start on the annual herd. One middle-aged man said he was only going to Tahoe, as he had to finish another trail in the Rocky Mountains and then take on some trail in Arizona. His plan was to hike 3,000 miles this year, which is almost ten times as far as I plan to hike. Most of these folk expect to be at the Canadian border by

mid to late September.

We also stopped to admire a massive, old Juniper, one that begged to be climbed, with limbs seductively close together. It turns out that the miners from the nineteenth century used the berries to make bathtub gin, something to ease the pain of digging all day for a couple bucks worth of gold.

From the trailhead, the other direction drops down to other views of the Holcomb Valley and after a about three miles crosses the Van Dusan Canyon Road, the main route into Holcomb Valley. For the day hiker, the stretch through Big Bear is an accessible part of the PCT, as there are several access points, allowing a hiker to sample sections of the trail without a full backpack.

For the backpacker, Big Bear is also hiker-friendly. People routinely give these folks a lift into town where they descend on the restaurants with buffets and spend the night in the local hostel, a welcome respite from sleeping on the hard ground. In fact, at the place where the trail crosses Van Dusan Canyon, there were several groups along the road, waiting for a lift to town.

Another access point, and a very different section of trail, is right on Highway 18, about two miles east of Baldwin Lake, which is dry most of the time. The trail crossing is at the top of the grade, just before the road winds steeply down to the Lucerne

Valley. There's a very big turnout on the south side of the road, with room to park many cars. The trail leads up from the parking area, but rather than the forest a few miles west, this is high desert, with fewer, smaller trees, brush and rock outcroppings. From the junction at Van Dusan Canyon to Hwy 18 is about seven or eight miles of trail, along the ridge above Baldwin Lake.

At first this high desert section of trail is very rocky, but than it smoothes out as it climbs around some rock outcroppings. After about a half mile, the trail tops out and starts to drop again and turn toward the San Gorgonio Wilderness. At that point, I walked a few feet off the trail to the right where I could look down at Baldwin Lake and also to a small, populated valley to the south. Then I saw what looked like a path up the other side, so I hiked a hundred or so yards up to the top. From there I could see down into the wide Lucerne Valley and the bare, rocky hills beyond.

The Big Bear Discovery Center on North Shore Drive will give you a local trail map, and there are four places where you can park and access the trail.

If you go, plan to stay a few days. The Quail Cove Lakeside Lodge in Fawnskin and Cabins 4 Less in Big Bear Lake offer great accommodations at a reasonable price, and the area has some wonderful restaurants.

Getting there: Big Bear City is located in San Bernardino County at the intersection of Highways 38 and 18.

23. Revisiting Point Sal (Nov/Dec 2013)

The last time I visited Point Sal, one of California's most off the beaten track state parks, I drove to within a few yards of the beach. Admittedly, the road wasn't great at the time, perhaps seventeen or eighteen years ago, with drifts of sand that made my wheels slip on the narrow, winding road. The road washed out in 1998, and now the only way to get there is on foot.

Fast forward to 2013. I remember the incredible look of the place and was obsessed with seeing it again. This is probably the only place on the California Coast where the shoreline makes a 90 degree turn and runs straight out for several miles before bending north again. Also, the point juts almost straight up for at least 1,200 feet to the top of the ridge.

Between pure curiosity and the need to update my travel book, I drove down Highway One past the town of Guadalupe to Brown Road and turned right. After three miles, the road ended at a gate with a sign indicating the Point Sal trail. The trail, in this case, is what's left of the old road, which actually doesn't look much worse than it did in the mid-1990s. Making sure I had plenty of water—none being available along the trail—I started out under a mix of blue and foggy skies.

The road climbs slightly until the first big curve, where it doubles back on itself and starts a fairly steep, two mile climb to the ridge top. For a good part of the way, I could look down at my car, looking smaller and smaller with each look.

Interestingly enough, on this hiking trip, I encountered quite a few others, while when I could still drive it, I was always on the road and beach totally alone.

All along the way, side trails branched off, each with a sign saying "Private property. No trespassing." The signs also said that violators would be cited, so I resisted the urge to explore off trail. Apparently, all the land along the route is either private or part of Vandenberg AFB, and only a small piece of the point is actually state land.

The terrain is mostly steep, grass-covered hills, with occasional stands of trees, except down in the gullies where small streams produce a green riparian corridor.

After doubling back where I could look down on the parking area, the road curved upward toward the ridge and the line of fog over the ocean. After a couple miles of climbing, the road crossed over an old, and now filled in, cattle grate. At that point, the top of the hill was just ahead.

Then the road drops again, turns to the right and climbs slightly along the side of the hill, and at one point there's a bit of an ocean view, and just ahead is a tall gate.

The gate is at the highest point on the trail. It's the entrance to Vandenberg AFB, with a sign that also warns that dog teams patrol the area. From that point until reaching the beach, the hiker is walking on the base.

While I wasn't particularly interested on hiking all the way down to the beach, I did envision hiking out along the ridge to the end of the point, believing there was an actual trail out there. Just past the gate, I learned otherwise. The path, more an improvised trail had another of those signs indicating that it was private property and citations would be issues. Apparently, that has not stopped some people who have hopped the barbed wire

fence and continued on, but it put a damper on my plans.

There was something compelling about the possibility of walking out to the fog-shrouded point, over the ridge line that went up and down like a sharp-edged saw blade.

A short walk down the trail, which now was dropping steeply, offered several great places to view the point and beach. The island, about three quarters of the way to the end of the point was intermittently visible through the shifting fog, and at no point on my hike could I see the end of the point. However, the beach directly below me was in full sunlight, with the bright blue water lapping on the sand. It looked almost inviting enough to warrant the additional two plus miles each way.

However, after walking down the trail a bit further, where I could see the road twist in loops down to the beach, past some AFB buildings, I had second thoughts. The trail down is much steeper—more elevation, less distance— than the one up from the parking area, and as it turned out, all of the half dozen parties I encountered along the way were only going as far as the view, about three miles hike from the trailhead. Also, once at the bottom, there's only a small beach. The shoreline along the point is bluffs and impassible, and everything south of the small beach is AFB property.

A short, steep climb brought me back to the gate and the

walk back. One interesting thing about the return trip was the view east, beyond the dry hills to the green, fertile flatlands near Santa Maria, the wide flood plain of the Santa Maria River, rich with crops.

After a six miles hike, I still had dreams of actually seeing the point, so I drove north on Highway One to Guadalupe and turned left on Main Street (166) for the 4.8 miles to Guadalupe Dunes County Park. The road ends at a parking lot at the beach. During the summer the dunes are cordoned off for the nesting plovers, but people are free to hike the beach. So I started south toward Mussel Rock, almost two miles away, through soft beach sand and blowing fog.

I had read that it's possible to go over Mussel Rock and down to Paradise Beach and on to the point. The problem is that getting over Mussel Rock requires climbing a 500 foot, steep sand dune, one that even the athletic, young county ranger was reluctant to do. Even should one make the climb, getting to the point, just as from the trail, is only possible by trespassing over private land. In short, a truly determined person can get out to the point, but only with great difficulty and the risk of a citation.

So, part of the mystery and draw of Point Sal is the

elusive point, rarely visible and very hard to reach.

Getting there: From Highway 101 at Nipomo at the south end of San Luis Obispo County, take Willow Rd. west to Hwy. 1 and go left through Guadalupe to Brown Rd, or from Santa Maria, north end of Santa Barbara County, take 166 west (Main Street) to Hwy. 1 at Guadalupe and turn left to Brown Rd, then right to end.

24. Hidden Gem: Byrne-Milliron Forest (Jan/Feb 2014)

According to some of the people I hiked with that late summer day, even some of the long-time local Sierra Club hike leaders

don't know this place. It doesn't show on most maps of parks and open spaces, and it's rather out of the way. It is, however, a lovely place to hike, with some stunning views to reward the person willing to take on a steep trail or two.

These 420 acres of redwood and mixed hardwood forest, with ten miles of trails and roads is the property of the Land Trust of Santa Cruz County, and it's somewhat of an island surrounded by private property.

The mile road up to the forest is one lane and marked for 10MPH. At the end of the road there's a dry, dirt parking lot that holds more than a dozen cars and belies the lush landscape that starts just up the trail. Starting at elevation about 850 feet, we started up the fire road to the left of the parking lot. At the gate there are informational brochures with trail maps. This fire road is the Byrne Trail, and it climbs steadily, gaining over 100 feet, through a redwood and hardwood mixed forest, keeping mostly in the shade, which was appreciated on that hot day.

After nearly a mile, we found a single track trail leading

steeply down to the right, the well-signed Leonard Bartle Trail. We quickly descended into a thick forest of redwoods, madrones and ferns, carefully making our way down until we crossed a small creek.

After climbing out of the creek, we started up the trail, now picking our way up the steep trail, an aerobic workout that caused our large group to spread out, mountain hoppers up front, butt draggers to the rear. Part way up we stopped at the "Cathedral Rest Stop." There was a bench and a rock with all kinds of trinkets and geodes left on it. It looked like some sort of memorial, but to whom or to what, I have no idea.

After a breather, we followed the twisting trail through deep shade, along the creek and under the redwoods, until we reached

the Byrne Trail again. Then we continued to climb until we topped out at about 1300 feet.

It looked like it would be all downhill from there, but after a short descent, we saw the Ridge Top Trail, a single track, rising straight up the hill on the right. Our leader turned, and we knew we were in for another workout, requiring frequent stops to catch our breath.

This trail, mostly in the shade, climbed even more steeply than the other single track, in places requiring careful footing to avoid slipping. At about 1600 feet, the trail burst out of the woods, and we found ourselves at "Eagle in the Tree" vista, a place with a picnic bench and views of Corralitos, part of the Pajaro Valley, the Moss Landing power plant and the distant hills near Carmel. To our delight, Jeff Helmer, the caretaker had left a basket of

freshly picked apples for hikers to enjoy.

Just before the top, we encountered one of several side trails that lead to private property, all signed to that effect. This one added the warning that there were guard dogs. Enough said.

We thought this was the lunch stop, but our hike leader said there was a better place a bit further, so we started down another fire road, the Ridge Top Road and soon discovered it was more than a bit further. At one point, a single track went off to the right, an alternate short cut to our next stop. I checked it out, but there was a section so steep a rope ran along the trail for about sixty yards, the rope is necessary for navigating the trail. We took the longer, less steep fire road. At a road junction, we went right in error, but soon realized our mistake. We were supposed to go straight.

It seemed like we'd lost a lot of elevation when we arrived AJ's Point of View, but we were still at 1300 feet, with views just as stunning as those at Eagle in the Tree. AJ's had a picnic table, several wooden chairs, and even two chairs just for small children. Interestingly, there was also a wooden teeter totter, which two of the ladies had fun with.

This was the lunch stop, with plenty of room for all nineteen of us. We also found another basket of apples, again much appreciated.

From there, we walked a few steps further down and found a sign with an arrow, saying "Parking." That went off to the right.

Going straight would have taken us back to the Byrne Trail, below where we turned off to the ridge top.

I was glad that this was the end, rather than the beginning of the hike, as this trail, actually a fire road, was very steep, with no flat spots to provide a rest. After a short way, the trail branched,

and both continue down, meeting up further down.

Nearly back down, a trail branched to the right, the sign saying "Parking." The other direction to the bottom of the Byrne Trail, a slightly longer way back.

Had we continued down that "wrong" trail above AJ's, we would have ended up at the Milliron Rest Spot. From there the Milliron Trail continues to the one other single track, the Great White Loop, which leads to the 233 foot tall "Great White" Redwood Tree, my destination on the next visit. After all, a white redwood is a rare thing, and I've only seen two others, both quite stunted, so a great one fascinates me.

Getting there is a bit tricky. From Highway One, heading south from Santa Cruz, take Freedom Blvd. and drive five miles to the stop sign at Corralitos Road. Turn left and go two miles to Browns Valley Road. There's the famous Corralitos Store and meat market there, so pick up some sausages or bacon on your way back. Browns Valley goes to the right, and at a stop sign it turns to the left. After a couple of miles of fairly open rural road, Browns Valley enters the canyon and redwood forest. Keep going, but look carefully to the left. At the sign for "Roses of

Yesterday," you turn left. Roses of Yesterday will be to the right, and there is a trail from there up to Byrne Forest. This is where the narrow road starts, and the forest's address is 809. Drive slowly around the blind curves.

If you are coming from the south, the Monterey area, exit Airport Blvd. in Watsonville, and turn left on Freedom, and then right on Corralitos, and follow directions above.

25. Tolowa Dunes: Little known state park (March/Apr. 2014)

Tucked away in the extreme northwest corner of California, a large and diverse state park suffers from a lack of visitors. Tolowa Dunes State Park surrounds Lake Earl just north of Crescent City and stretches from the edge of the city to the mouth of the Smith River, some eleven miles north. The park has thirty miles of official trails, often intersected by others that don't show on the map.

Sadly, most Californians aren't aware of the park, so most of the visitors are locals, taking their afternoon hikes or walking their dogs. It's not unusual to have a trail all to yourself, even on a summer weekend. Actually, summer doesn't mean quite the same thing up here. It can be either warm and sunny in the summer or foggy and windy. The same is pretty much true the rest of the year. Sure, it rains often in the winter, but when it's not raining, it could be a perfect day.

Tolowa Dunes offers a variety of hiking experiences, including lush meadows, wetlands, lakes and ponds, thick forests and rolling sand dunes. The only thing it doesn't offer is killer hills, being mostly flat. However, if you need that aerobic workout, walking up and down the dunes will do it for you.

There is even an eleven mile stretch of the California Coastal Trail, one of several segments in the county. If you drive out Washington Blvd from Crescent City to the beach and turn right on Radio Road, you'll be in the Point St. George Heritage Area. From the lot, you can access the trail, which runs along the beach all the way to the mouth of the Smith River. There are two other parking areas along the way, along with four other trails leading inland. This is one of the few places left where you can walk for hours along wild, undeveloped beaches. However, due to the afternoon winds, it would be best to tackle this early in the morning to avoid blowing sand.

Instead of turning on Washington, you can continue north on Northcrest Drive and make a left on Old Mill Road, which ends at the visitor center and access to several delightful trails. Also, just before the visitor center, Sand Hill Road goes off to the left and ends at another parking area and trail head, which is probably a good place to start our exploration.

From this dirt parking area, the 3 mile Dead Lake round trip trail heads south through a large meadow, bordered by trees. After .4 mile, at Sweetwater Creek, the trail goes either left or right. The right trail follows little Sweetwater Creek toward the beach, where you can make a four mile loop back to the parking area through dunes, meadows and forests. The left fork is the way to Dead Lake, a beautiful and poorly-named small body of water. This trail goes through a lovely wood, parallels the north shore of the lake and ends at the South Big Dune, which looks like a mini version of the Sahara Desert. However long before the end of the trail, there is a narrow trail to the right that leads down to the lake, with just enough room for four or five people to stand. There are flowering plants growing out of that end of the lake, and looking across the lake you'll spot a boat dock. Yes you can drive there from the other side on Riverside Drive. Back at the parking lot, the trail that goes to the right from the parking lot is the one that is part of the beach and Sweetwater Creek loop. Also, as in most trails here, along this loop you'll find a side trail that leads off to the next hike.

Park at the visitor center, which may or may not be open, and either take the gravel road or the single track trail to the right. They both access the same network of trails. The main trail is the Cadra Point Loop, 4.2 miles, plus whatever side trails you wish to explore. This gravel road runs through a lush forest, and Lake Earl is to the right and can be accessed at several places. The first, about a half mile in, is the unmarked Alder Marsh Trail, a narrow path that leads to the edge of the lake. There is no clear line between land and lake on this side, the trail leading to soft, damp ground and then to a shallow marsh. The main trail leads to Cadra Point, about a mile in, an ideal place to watch the flocks of local birds, and another place where land meets marsh.

Continuing on, a side trail leads to Goose Point, another good place to view Lake Earl and the distant mountains. Actually, Lake Earl and the smaller Lake Tolowa are the same body of water, separated by a narrows, which you can reach on this hike. After returning to the main trail from Goose Point, a short walk leads to a junction at McLaughlin Pond, a marshy extension of lake Tolowa. To complete the 4.2 mile hike, turn left. To add another two mile round trip, go right to the end, where the "two" lakes meet. On the other side is a place to launch a boat or kayak.

On the return trip, you'll pass Beaver Pond and the side trail to the dunes and Sweetwater Creek.

Once back to the parking lot and ready for another short hike, drive back to Northcrest and make a left. It becomes Lake Earl Drive. After you pass Lakeview Drive and then Elk Valley Cross

Road, look for parking on the left. This is a short, just over a mile, round trip, starting with a meadow before entering a forest. Then the trail branches into a loop. At the far end of the loop there is a nice view of Lake Earl, complete with a marshy shore and lots of birds, flowers and butterflies. It was on this trail that I noticed a tiny, green tree frog on a sword-like leaf, by the side of the trail.

There is a northern part of the park, an area I haven't really explored, an area of dunes, small ponds and access to the mouth of the Smith River. The best place to start this exploration is to turn left off Lake Earl Drive on to Lower Lake Drive and continue about five miles to the end at Pala Road, where you can only go left. Pala ends about a half mile at the parking area. There are restrooms, and the trail heads west through a meadow. When you reach the River Trail, you can head right to the Smith River or left to the Horse Camp, Ridge Trail and the small ponds.

You can download a map of the trail system at *http://www.tolowacoasttrails.org/trails.html*

This park can be seen on foot, by bike, on horseback or by kayak, and there's enough here for several days of exploration. All these trailheads can be accessed by taking Hwy. 101 through Crescent City, and making a left on Northcrest Dr., a major intersection at the north end of downtown.

26. The pride (and views) of San Luis Obispo (May/June 2014)

It seemed
to me that
every out-
door lover
in the San
Luis
Obispo
and Pismo
Beach area
got glassy-
eyed at the
mention of
Bishop Peak, located just beyond the San Luis Obispo city limits.
Apparently, this is the locals' favorite hike, the one they all recommend. This peak is the tallest of the Nine Sisters, that string of
volcanic Morros that stretch from San Luis Obispo to Morro
Rock in Morro Bay. There are two trailheads, one at the end of
Highland Drive, and another at Patricia Drive, which involves a
longer hike.

I opted for Highland Drive, and since it was a cool day
and the round trip only 3.5 miles, I didn't bother to take water. I
didn't consider the 950 foot elevation gain in the 1.75 mile assent
and that walking in the sun over rocks kicks the temperature up.
Even though it was late November, I was pretty hot and thirsty
by the time I reached the top, but the views made me forget any
discomfort.

On the hike I passed or was passed by dozens of people,
almost all young, fit and thin, likely students from Cal Poly, visible from the top of the peak. Seeing these college kids hopping
from rock to rock made me feel my age.

At the end of Highland Drive there is parking on the
street. The start of the trail is marked by an open space sign, and

as I started along the trail, I could see the peak, like a massive rock hat, directly above me. Soon, I was passing a long fence separating the open space from private dwellings. This was a lovely, wooded stretch, no more than a quarter mile long.

The woods ended at open grassland and a fence. I looked left and saw more fences, so I mistakenly turned right and followed the trail around, picking up the Felsman Loop Trail, coming up from Patricia Drive and adding another quarter mile to the hike. I soon discovered that I should have turned left at the fence and followed the wide trail steeply up, past a water tank and on to a gate with signage, a gate I erroneously approached from the other direction.

Going through the gate, the Felsman Loop Trail is to the right, and the Bishop trail is left. It rises steeply through the grassy meadow, and just before it enters the woods, there's a narrow single track trail going off to the right. That leads to a rock climbing spot. The main trail goes straight into the woods before curving left and climbing for a short distance along the shoulder of the peak.

Then the trail drops again for a couple hundred yards before starting up again. Soon the woods end at the rocky and difficult part of the trail. From this point to the top, the trail is very rocky, with sections that require scampering up rocks and rock steps. This can feel dicey if one isn't sure-footed.

I realized I'd left the hill portion behind and I was on the morro. As the trail wrapped around the east side of Bishop Peak, I went from looking straight down on San Luis Obispo to some great views of Cerro San Luis, the smaller morro to the east. Then a series of switchbacks and rock steps brought me around to the south side of the peak, and I realized how steep the sides of Bishop Peak really are. This is essentially a very large rock that has been broken up over countless millennia, and the trail was more rock that dirt.

Once on the south side of the peak, the summit was continually visible directly above me, and I could see people standing on the massive boulder at the top. This was where it got hot and I got thirsty. Seeing the college students in tank tops and shorts, I realized I was, in long pants and a sweatshirt, overdressed for this climb, but it was too late to go back and change.

The top was above me, but the trail was a series of switchbacks, often narrow and requiring stepping from boulder to boulder.

I almost did not realize I'd reached the top, until I saw the benches with people having lunch. A jagged spine of rock extends a bit higher, making it seem like I wasn't quite there yet. The top of the trail is a saddle between two sections of rocky spine. However at the top, a few more steps and I could look down the north slope at Highway One and Cal Poly beyond. There were two benches and plenty of rocks to sit on. However, the actual top was about twenty feet higher, atop that huge boulder I'd been watching as I climbed. Getting on top of it requires actual rock climbing and is better done with a partner, so I went part way and turned back. Beside, being hot and thirsty, I'd already had my share of climbing and was ready to get back down.

Going back, while less tiring, requires more care. A fall on the rocks could be very painful and possibly bone breaking, so I took my time, unlike the trail runner who shot past me. Also, the stunning views are continual on the descent, making it hard to watch your footing, and, whatever else can be said about this hike, it's certainly all about the views. The only view I didn't get was directly west, toward Morro Bay, which I might have gotten a look at had I climbed that last boulder.

The return trip is almost all downhill, except for that one section along the wooded northern flank, which when you're tired, suddenly feels longer than a couple hundred yards. This time I went through the gate and down to the trail junction, for that short walk through the woods back to the car.

The Patricia Drive parking area is somewhat lower, and the trail, which runs through sloping meadows, is somewhat longer. However, all that rock hopping made my feet sore, and I was more than glad to get the boots off. I wasn't sorry I missed the Felsman Loop Trail.

Getting there: Take highway 101 in San Luis Obispo to the Highway One exit, and head toward Morro Bay. After three or four signals, and just after passing the city limits, there's a light and a left turn lane at Highland Drive. Turn left and continuing winding up the hill until Highland ends. At one intersection on Highland, there's a sign pointing toward the Patricia Dr. parking area.

Tan Bark Trail: Big Sur at its Best (July/August, 2014)

Almost anyone who has seen the Big Sur Coast agrees that it is one of world's majestic places. Each trail into the brush and each pullout offers unique scenes. One need only hike in a few minutes to be in what seems another world.

One of my favorite Big Sur hikes was closed for a long time due to the 2008 fire, but happily, it is open again. This half day, over six mile hike is visually stunning and emotionally therapeutic, a perfect place to eliminate stress.

The Tan Bark Trail to the old Tin House is in the center of the Big Sur coast. The trail head is a Partington Canyon just south of milepost 38 on Highway 1 and just across the road from Partington Cove.

Within 50 yards of the parking spot the trail enters a wonderland, suddenly shifting from open coastal to a dense redwood forest and then to a bridge over frothy, tumbling Partington creek. The canyon, only a couple dozen yards wide in spots, is thickly wooded and the ambient light is muted green and burnt sienna, and everything seems soft and damp and cool. The creek cascades over rocks and fallen logs in a series of rapids and waterfalls. Every inch of the creek is dynamic and fascinating, making it hard to watch the trail as it climbs along the side of this musical flow of white water.

In some places the walls on both sides are bare rock, stretching up in a steep "V," dripping with hanging moss and ferns. The permanent dampness pervades all of the senses.

That first half mile or so is as beautiful as any place I have ever been. Once you've walked it, whenever someone mentions "redwood canyon," the lower Tan Bark trail will immediately come to mind. One could spend hours lazily exploring that short stretch. There are numerous places to step off the trail and down to a rock at creek side, to sit and watch the little waterfalls or perhaps take a photo.

A bit more than a half mile in, the trail abruptly turns away from the creek and starts to climb up the canyon wall. The trail is wet from the tiny feeder creeks that trickle down the canyon. In a steep section, you leave the canyon floor and climb high on the canyon side, and the trail levels out again. Up on the high southern edge of the canyon the forest becomes mixed and sunny, tanbark oaks mixing with redwoods. It heads back toward the highway again, and before it turns sharply inland again, you can climb a few feet up a side trail and look down at the highway and the ocean. However, while the trail has seen extensive restoration after the fire, this side trail ends in thick brush, making it hard to get to the view. After heading inland again, the trail turns right into a redwood forest, as it climbs high above the south fork of the creek. The trail runs along the steep side of the canyon, and each time you pause, the water music whispers from below.

Near the top of the canyon the trail crosses the creek near the headwaters, where it becomes three narrow and gentle trickles. There, along the creek, at the junction of two branches of the south fork, in a grove of majestic old redwoods, there is a bench, made of a split redwood, just a few feet from the creek. The fire has scorched it, so bring a rag to sit on. Common courtesy among

the frequent hikers is, for the sake of solitude, if you have en-
joyed the bench for a time, move on when the next person comes
along, allowing him or her time to meditate on the natural world.

This is a solitary, reflective place, soothing and serene, bucolic and peaceful. A few minutes there is worth a week of meditation and yoga. It's a place that will bringyou're your inner artist
or poet.

Those in a hurry can return along the same path, but continuing a few minutes longer rewards the hiker with another magical
spot.

The trail continues upward for perhaps another 20 minutes,
out of the shaded redwood groves, into the mixed forest, with occasional ocean vistas. Then the trail turns downhill, and soon
merges with a fire road. A right turn leads steeply down the
wooded road to Highway One, and a ¾ mile walk along the highway back to the car.

Almost everyone, however, goes left for a quarter mile detour
to the old Tin House. The Tin House was built by a friend of
F.D.R. during World War Two, as a place where the President

could get away from it
all. F.D.R. never stayed
there, and the place,
closed up, and pretty
much a ruin since the
fire, now belongs to the
State.

To reach it, walk
down the fire road to
the left for a few dozen
yards, and then turn
sharply to the right for
a short, steep descent
to the Tin House.

While the house it-
self is of historical in-
terest, the real reward
to the hiker hides be-

hind the house. There is a beautiful meadow that slopes down and then drops sharply away to the sea. This is the place to pull off the day pack, unpack the lunch, and enjoy a sweeping view of the best of the Big Sur coast.

If you are taking this hike in the spring, that meadow is green, fragrant and filled with flowers. Also, the shaded part of the lower section of the fire road,

just above the highway, will be ablaze in wildflowers. If you go in the heat of late spring or early summer, bring insect repellent. The flies and gnats can be fierce. The upside is that the warm weather brings out thousands of butterflies that can become so thick that the air in front of you appears to dance like heat waves in the desert.

You can look toward the famous McWay waterfall at Julia Pfeiffer Beach, once you are back on the highway. There is a scenic pull out across the road from the bottom of the fire road.

Take care walking back, as the shoulder is narrow, wider on the ocean side, which offers glimpses of crashing waves. Or, if you come with friends, bring two cars and leave one at the scenic pull out, thus avoiding an unappealing one mile walk on the road.

The hiker on a tight schedule can make the loop in three and a half hours. For a leisurely walk and lunch, allow four or five.

Other books by Meade Fischer

With the Sea Beside Me:An intimate guide to California's central and north coast: A complete coastal guide for the adventur traveler from Santa Barbara to the Oregon border, including camping, hiking, kayaking, back roads and hidden beaches, plus places to stop for food drink and lodging.

Cosmic Coastal Chronicle:A solitary wanderer travels the west coast from Big Sur to British Columbia. searching for surf, kayaking spots, hiking trails, interesting people and some insights into the great mysteries of life. Lost in a world of peace and beauty, he both celebrates and learns the lessons of life. (non fiction)

Shattering the Crystal Face of God: A spiritual cynic searches for personal truth and meaning in encounters with nature and the lessons of the spontaneous. (non fiction)

Spinning Real Life: In this satire, an idealistic young writersets out to write about real life and gets hopelessly emeshed in it, as world-changing events unfold around him and the women in his life are always one step ahead of him. (fiction)

Messiah Chronicles: The Jesus story, sans the miracles.A religious reformer, with his band of followers, travels ancient Judea, preaching religious reform, which angers some segments of his society.A Roman centurian takes a liking to himand tries to protect him, while keeping the peace.

A Grand Plan: A young girl's seven year plan for a literary career and an obsession to marry her mentor and teacher, and her attempt to get him to share her vision.

The Boy from Tomorrow: a boy from the future learns to cope with the primative 21st century.

Coming in 2015: To Sea for Myself: Reflections of a solitary kayaker.

www.baymoon.com/~eclecticpress

eclecticpress@baymoon.com

Or, search for Meade Fischer on amazon.com

www.ingramcontent.com/pod-product-compliance
Lightning Source LLC
Chambersburg PA
CBHW060114050426
42448CB00010B/1865